Liberal Education and the National Curriculum

Liberal Education and the National Curriculum

David Conway

Civitas: Institute for the Study of Civil Society
London

First Published January 2010

© Civitas 2010
77 Great Peter Street
London SW1P 2EZ
Civitas is a registered charity (no. 1085494)
and a company limited by guarantee, registered in
England and Wales (no. 04023541)

email: books@civitas.org.uk

ISBN 978-1-906837-11-2

Typeset by
Civitas

Printed in Great Britain by
The Cromwell Press Group
Trowbridge, Wiltshire

Contents

Author

David Conway received his education at St Olave's Grammar School, Clare College Cambridge and University College London.

He taught for over three decades at Middlesex University, of which he is an Emeritus Professor of Philosophy, before joining Civitas as a Senior Research Fellow in 2004.

His previous publications include *A Farewell to Marx*, *Classical Liberalism*, *Free-Market Feminism*, *The Rediscovery of Wisdom*, *In Defence of the Realm*, *A Nation of Immigrants?* and *Disunited Kingdom*.

Acknowledgements

I should like to thank several of my colleagues at Civitas for various different varieties of help during the writing of this publication.

In particular, I should like to thank its Director David Green for agreeing to my suggestion that I write a publication on this topic for Civitas and for his patience while I did; Deputy Director Robert Whelan, for his customary meticulous copy-editing and numerous other kindnesses; Director of Education and Family Policy, Anastasia de Waal, for being always ready to provide useful information when I have sought it from her; and Nicholas Cowen for many lively and productive conversations about education over the years.

I should also like to thank the anonymous referees whose helpful suggestions have done so much to improve the book.

Foreword

All political labels tend to become misleading over time, as the circumstances which gave rise to them change out of all recognition and recede from memory; and it is obvious that certain terms remain in continuous use while undergoing a gradual but fundamental change of meaning. Individuals, too, without any conscious alteration in their political commitments, can find their relationship to the wider world subverted by events. As Hannah Arendt remarked: 'The most radical revolutionary will become a conservative on the day after the revolution',[1] while the same revolution, presumably, will turn conservatives into radicals.

Nowhere is this truer than in the politics of education. In speaking of 'progressive' ideas, 'child-centred' pedagogy, 'traditional academic subjects' or a 'liberal education', we are using terms whose meanings have shifted over time, and which often convey quite different things to different people. Similarly, while the names of certain public exams and subject areas have remained fairly constant—so that, for instance, one can still sit an English, history or physics A-level—their substantive content and form has changed radically, especially over the last couple of decades.

In *Liberal Education and the National Curriculum*, David Conway offers an antidote to this state of linguistic and political confusion. By tracing the origins of the National Curriculum to the liberal educational reformers of the nineteenth and early twentieth century, he places it— and by extension those who oppose it—in an intelligible historical and political context. The story starts with Matthew Arnold's project of making a liberal education generally available to English children, where necessary by harnessing the coercive power of the state—a personal commitment which arose from his work as an inspector of schools in England, and which he expounded at length in *Culture and Anarchy*, published in 1869.

The urgency of this programme arose from the acute and multi-faceted crisis of England in Arnold's day. Urbanisation and industrialisation had provoked massive migration within the United Kingdom, destroying the traditional culture of rural communities, and destabilising the family life on which the successful education of the young ultimately depends. At the same time, through Disraeli's Reform Act of

1867, the franchise was being extended to working men for the first time, placing on them a responsibility which clearly demanded a high level of intellectual and moral formation.

Arnold argued that if this combination of cultural impoverishment, along with growing economic and political power, was not to precipitate a major disaster, energetic and imaginative reform was needed, especially in the realm of education. Yet it seemed to him that those responsible for education in England were peculiarly unlikely to rise to the occasion. During his work as an inspector, he had acquired a horror of the provincialism and narrowness of many teachers, and spoke of the 'prison of Puritanism' which had blighted even the elite intellectual and cultural life of England since the mid-seventeenth century.

In order to block and outmanoeuvre these forces, Arnold demanded that the state must take responsibility for the education of children from the poor and middling classes, and that they should be given a broad liberal education. As Conway shows, Arnold's proposed curriculum was, in all essentials, that which he had admired in his visits to schools in France and Prussia, and which subsequent reformers over the next century and more have sought to shore up and maintain; and it was to all intents and purposes this scheme which was introduced as the National Curriculum by Kenneth Baker's 1988 Education Reform Act.

From the perspective of our own time, perhaps the most striking thing about the history of liberal education from Arnold to Baker is the degree of agreement it gave rise to. Revolutionary as well as democratic socialists, High Tories and liberal conservatives, Anglicans, Roman Catholics, Dissenters and secular humanists were in agreement that a child in a complex, democratic and liberal society ought to be given an education broadly of the kind envisaged by Arnold and his successors. Naturally there were those who argued for more emphasis on science or art within the curriculum, or who wanted more time for modern languages; but there was surprisingly little disagreement about the importance of the core academic subjects as the essential catalysts for the intellectual, imaginative and spiritual development of every child.

The situation today could hardly be more different. As Conway shows, those who defend liberal education are now in a small minority among the educational establishment at all levels, from the department of state official to the primary school teacher. The conventional view among local and central government officials, education academics and teachers is that children will not benefit from, let alone enjoy, being introduced to the complex patterns of knowledge which comprise traditional subjects such as history (especially military and political history), physics, or the grammar of English and other languages. On the contrary, according to John White, emeritus professor of philosophy at London University's Institute of Education, these forms of knowledge are 'a middle-class creation... whose effect... has been to make it difficult for many children... to adjust to a highly academic school culture...' (p. 11).[2] While in the words of Martin Johnson, acting general secretary of the Association of Teachers and Lecturers (ATL), 'most people are not intellectuals' and therefore cannot benefit from a 'curriculum considered necessary for social elites' in the nineteenth and early twentieth centuries (p. 12).[3]

Instead of exposing children to such intellectual challenges, and incidentally demanding of teachers that they master and transmit complex bodies of knowledge with clarity, imagination and enthusiasm, many educationists argue that we should elevate 'experience' and 'feelings' over the more or less abstract forms of knowledge associated with academic subjects. Not only is academic knowledge too difficult for most children (according to these writers), but the understanding of objective matters which it gives rise to encourages a critical, disinterested and solitary frame of mind, whereas children should be steered by their teachers towards 'self-conscious social and political objectives'.[4]

This double objection to the rigorous academic content of liberal education—that it is too difficult for most children, and that children who have gained a level of mastery in such an education are apt to form politically uncooperative cultural or knowledge elites—is not new. The belief that most people are incapable of benefiting from a liberal education has been a characteristic of ultra-conservative thinkers in all ages (a point I will return to); while the emphasis on the importance of cultivating feelings instead of (rather than in combination with, and subject to) a habit of disinterested thought, also has long antecedents, going back at least to the Romantic view that the principal aim of education is the full development of the sentiments.

As Conway makes clear, the influential advocates of liberal education, heirs, after all, to the Romantic tradition, have shared this concern with the cultivation of aesthetic and emotional experience—

indeed, it often appears to be their motivating principle. In the view of Arnold himself, as well as his influential successors such as Cyril Norwood, T.S. Eliot and Kenneth Baker, an education which failed to develop a child's subjective response to art, literature and life would certainly be a failure. Yet, as a moment's thought reveals, it is quite wrong to suppose that one's imaginative and aesthetic responses arise only in opposition to intellect and reason, or that cultivating the intellect will weaken a child's emotional capacities. Indeed, this way of thinking seems to betray a positively Puritanical view of human nature as fundamentally flawed and alienated—a view which has particularly disturbing implications in the context of education.

Rather, the liberal educational tradition seeks to develop the capacity for subjective response through a child's active intellectual and imaginative engagement with complex and worthwhile material. By concentrating largely on the transmission of objective bodies of knowledge, and by directing his or her enthusiasm and attention mainly to these, rather than to the pupil's developing response, the liberal educator allows children the freedom to contemplate, explore and respond—or not to respond—in their own time and way, as a result of an interior process which cannot be forced or pre-empted. By contrast, the child-centred approach, which takes the child's responses and interests as its starting point, and in which the presentation of materials from outside the child's experience is considered damaging, removes the veil of privacy from the child's subjectivity, and places pressure on him or her to respond—or pretend to respond—in public, according to a predetermined set of expectations.

This process can easily become manipulative and invasive from the child's point of view, and it is hardly surprising if some children respond to it with hostility, or by withdrawing their cooperation.

Where the presentation of information is motivated by the desire that children should feel and respond in a certain way, there is a danger that teaching will descend into propaganda. Indeed the totalitarian regimes of the twentieth century tended to regard education as the means of cultivating certain stereotypical emotional responses (which could easily be pressed into political service), while deprecating the traditional concern with knowledge and intellectual judgement, which could only result in an enhanced capacity for criticism and dissent. Reflecting on the Nazi Party's destruction of the classical curriculum in the German gymnasia during his own schooldays, one particularly able classicist has remarked: 'In retrospect it seems to me that an education in Greek and Latin antiquity created a mental attitude that resisted seduction by a totalitarian ideology.'[5] Clearly, people are much easier to manipulate and direct if they have never formed the habit of subjecting their experience and feelings to critical examination, and if their responses are not grounded in wide reading and deep reflection. Such independently minded, well educated individuals are always among the first victims of totalitarianism.

By contrast, and at the risk of stating the obvious, a liberal society with a constitutional, representative form of government, and prizing a high degree of personal liberty, requires as many thoughtful, independently minded citizens as it can possibly have. A free society cannot operate without a large body of well educated citizens, who have the ability and confidence to hold the government and public servants generally to account. This was Arnold's view, and it remains true 140 years later: children (and everyone else) in a free society need to gain a reasonable degree of mastery over their feelings, appetites and behaviour if they are to enjoy any degree of happiness personally, or contribute to maintaining a decent and humane society. To imagine that the intellectual habits and understanding required by such a society can be left to develop spontaneously is a delusion. The power of regarding all questions, even those that touch one's own interests, with a degree of disinterest; a positive desire to see things from other people's points of view; an observant scepticism, even irony, in relation to one's own responses and predispositions; the refusal to join in with bullying; the demand that an argument should be not just popular, but honest and fair-minded; a refusal to engage in moral grandstanding or emotional blackmail; a wide knowledge of history and literature, and of the traditions of thought which make existing institutions and customs comprehensible—these accomplishments and character traits demand a careful and persistent effort of encouragement on the part of teachers and parents, as well as hard work by children, if they are to remain sufficiently common to allow a liberal society to survive.

Even so, and having accepted the vital importance of re-establishing a liberal curriculum, one has to admit that such a programme confronts enormous difficulties. Critics of the liberal educational tradition are entitled to point out that there is a large divergence among its influential advocates as to how optimistic one should be about the educability of the population as a whole. John White, Martin Johnson and the other authors quoted by Conway are not the only people who have doubted whether pupils of average or less than average ability, or with ability but little desire to learn, will ever gain the necessary mastery of complex material necessary for any real enjoyment of traditional subjects. Pessimism of this kind was one of the considerations which led conservative defenders of classical education such as T.S. Eliot to oppose attempts to compel all children to receive it: Eliot feared that the attempt to give *everyone* such an education, regardless of ability, would result in a watering down of the curriculum and eventually a situation of complete failure, in which *nobody*—not even the most able—any longer had the opportunity to participate in a really rigorous classical education.[6]

As David Conway makes clear, however, and as we have already seen, a liberal education is not aimed merely at the development of the intellect: there is also a consistent concern, common to all the advocates of liberal education he cites (and certainly including Eliot), with the growth of affective and aesthetic discernment, of moral character and judgement, as the receiving mind and imagination of the pupil grapples and comes to terms with the new objects of knowledge. This point is made by Newman at length in *The Idea of a University*; and it is something of an obsession with the English nineteenth-century novelists, who consistently ridiculed what they took to be the utilitarian conception of education, with its philistine insistence on measurable outcomes and the parroting of unconnected scraps of information.

Yet a critic of liberal education might object that this emphasis on the pupil's interior response to the materials of the liberal education—the energetic transformation of his thought and imagination as he comes into contact with worthwhile objects of study—does not in itself mean that it is going to be possible to educate children of all abilities. Indeed, it could be argued that this non-intellectual, imaginative and creative aspect of education raises further obstacles to the project of providing a liberal education to all children: something has to happen in the pupil's interior consciousness which *cannot be forced*. To use a theological analogy, the pupil must, through some combination of influences and a kind of intellectual or emotional openness, allow himself to be 'touched with grace'.

Moreover, so far as the humanities are concerned—at any rate beyond the primary school level—whether this interior response has occurred or not cannot be certified by a simple external test, but only by a fairly prolonged, conscious engagement between pupils and a person more fully educated than they are, in which the pupils demonstrate (perhaps unwittingly), either through writing an essay or in conversation, that their acquisition of knowledge is beginning to bear fruit in the form of disciplined and creative intelligence.

A pessimist could argue, therefore, that liberal education can only benefit children who are both intelligent and, in some way that cannot be measured or predicted, are also open to the experience of inner engagement; for even an intelligent person who is well instructed, under good psychological and ambient conditions, can still fail to acquire such an interior illumination and sound judgement, and can remain (as Newman says) unformed by the 'passive reception of scraps and details'.

There are two kinds of optimism in relation to the education debate, and they tend to cancel each other out. Eliot had high (by our present standards, phenomenally high) expectations of what liberal education should involve (which is one kind of optimism); and correspondingly few illusions about the possibility of making such an education available to all children (pessimism). Eliot's pessimism was not widely shared, however, and was not influential in official circles. Most of his contemporaries in the early and mid-twentieth century expected rather less of the curriculum (for example, they were willing to substitute English for Latin and Greek as the principal means of access to great literature), and so entertained correspondingly higher hopes for public education. It was their thinking which won the day until the 1960s, and this, as Conway argues, remains the best approach for contemporary advocates of a liberal education.

What is striking in this historical perspective is that contemporary educational theorists such as Johnson and White (quoted above) have become the heirs of Eliot's ultra-conservative pessimism about the educability of the mass of the population. Indeed, their pessimism is greater that Eliot's because, unlike him, they argue that many children are incapable of mastering even the simplified, mother-tongue liberal education of the Norwood Report and its successors. But is this deeply anti-progressive point of view justified?

There is a danger that the anti-progressive pessimism of White, Johnson and the contemporary educational establishment in general will serve as (or has already become) a self-fulfilling prophecy. The education of children in the liberal tradition requires a large body of educated adults willing to sacrifice their time and energy for future generations, not just as teachers and inspectors, but as supportive parents, politicians, intellectuals and so on. In short, it requires a reasonably coherent, confident and dominant *living culture* which to a sufficient extent embodies and manifests liberal educational values in society at large. The more ambitious the plans of educational reformers (e.g. to make a liberal education available to all children), the stronger and more widespread this culture needs to be. Conversely, in its absence, even a modest attempt to instil a liberal educational ethos in a minority of schools may quickly run up against a shortage of enthusiastic teachers or parents.

Since the contemporary educational establishment contains many people in positions of power who are avowedly hostile to a liberal education, it may be that we have already reached that limit. Under these circumstances, even if one accepts the optimistic attitude of J.S. Mill, Arnold and the twentieth-century reformers about the educability of most children, it may simply have become impossible to maintain an Arnoldian approach to public education because of the collapse of the public culture. The task for advocates of liberal education, then, is not just to change what is happening in British schools, but just as urgently, to build up an enthusiastic constituency for such a policy.

If liberal education is to become a popular cause among the general public, it will be important to demonstrate that such education is conducive to the intellectual and creative fulfilment of all kinds of children, especially the most disadvantaged; and that it is crucial to the progress and peaceful development of our complex society. Conversely, it needs to be stressed that the attacks on liberal education and traditional subjects are opposed to the interests of children, and to the cohesion of society in general. There are several points that deserve to be emphasised.

First, by amplifying and representing in a modern form the pessimism of ultra-conservative thinkers such as Eliot about the impossibility of giving a liberal education to the masses, the approach of the current educational establishment ensures that only a few privileged children will be exposed to the artistic and literary materials which have fed the life of the intellect and imagination in the West since ancient times. These fortunate children will have a vast and increasingly unbridgeable advantage in entering elite higher education and gaining positions of influence in society, exacerbating the diminishment of social mobility that has already taken place over the last several decades.

Secondly, an education carried out in accordance with current theories cannot be called 'progressive' or 'liberal' in any meaningful or positive sense of those words: that is, far from enriching children's lives and broadening their minds to fit them for a life of freedom and responsibility, such an approach can only serve to trap them in a narrow mental confinement. Why is this?

Conway quotes extensively from the writings of Richard Pring, former Professor of Educational Studies at the University of Oxford. Pring, who in this respect seems to be representative of the current establishment, maintains that the traditional canon is not liberating in itself, and that modern children in particular are bound to find it oppressive and incomprehensible. This being the case, one would expect him to propose a new canon, in the manner of those Bolsheviks in the early days of the Soviet Union who argued that the school curriculum based on the literature and scholarship of the pre-revolutionary era ought to be replaced with a new curriculum based on 'Prolecult'. Indeed, Pring does seem to be advocating this when he writes: 'the tradition of liberal education... writes off too many young people... Their voices are not allowed into the conversation, and the voices they listen to are not considered to be among "the best that has been thought or said"... Perhaps the tradition itself needs to be re-examined' (pp. 97-98).[7] Yet this suggestion is undercut by his subsequent statement that: 'There is not, nor will ever be, consensus over what literature is most worth reading...'; and that there is no possibility of 'moral expertise'(p. 98).[8] Rather than basing children's education on any coherent body of knowledge, therefore, let alone on a liberal arts and sciences curriculum drawn from a wide historic and cultural range, Pring is proposing that schooling should be based on the children's pre-existing knowledge of the here and now. Yet such an approach clearly involves a radical diminishment in the scope of each child's potential experience.

xv

By bringing them into contact with the experiences and knowledge of people of widely different and yet ultimately connected historic and cultural epochs, the liberal curriculum offers children of all backgrounds the chance of better comprehending, and even perhaps of mentally transcending, their own particular experiences, by learning to see their lives in the context of an overarching pattern of human achievement. In the absence of such an opportunity, each child is left isolated in the midst of his or her own experience, with no means to connect private impressions of the world with the wider experience of humanity. This deprivation is obviously damaging to the child in question, who is left in a profound intellectual and imaginative solitude. But it is also harmful to the cohesion, solidarity and goodwill necessary to society at large.

This last point is surely worth stressing. In many modern British schools, and especially those with high proportions of disadvantaged children, where few pupils speak English at home, and in which a great number of different minority groups are represented—some, for historic reasons, in a state of underlying hostility to one another—the idea that the teaching programme should be based on the experiences peculiar to each child is manifestly unworkable.

Indeed, there is good reason to believe that in a culturally and ethnically diverse country, it is *particularly* important to encourage attachment to a form of identity which is essentially political or civic (rather than tribal or ethnic) and which is capable of drawing children into a shared public culture. This appears to be the implication of recent investigations by Paul Collier and his colleagues into the relationship between ethnic diversity and the political process in East Africa. Collier's team found that in Tanzania, where Julius Nyerere (president from 1964 until 1984) had insisted on schools teaching in a single national language (Kiswahili), and using a curriculum which embodied 'a strong dose of pan-Tanzanian history', a powerful sense of Tanzanian identity has emerged. Responding to the question, 'Which specific group do you belong to first and foremost?', only three per cent replied by naming their tribe; a full 97 per cent described themselves as Tanzanians. By contrast, across the border in Kenya, a country with rather lower levels of tribal diversity, education has been left in the hands of local committees, and many schools teach in the tribal languages, making no coordinated attempt to transmit a national historical narrative or shared culture. Here the majority of people, when asked what group they belong to, gave the name of their tribe.[9]

These responses have stark implications for politics and society in the two countries, as the communal violence following the 2007 elections in Kenya made abundantly clear. It would be complacent to assume that Britain is inherently immune to the emergence of identity politics: the British National Party has begun to achieve a degree of electoral success which would have seemed out of the question even ten years ago; it is possible that other parties appealing to a racial or ethnic base may also start to gain significant followings, if only at a local level. Should Britain follow Tanzania's example, and establish an intelligent and coherent history curriculum for schools which emphasises the civil and political history of the UK? By teaching children about the development of our constitutional arrangements—i.e. by focusing on the traditional narrative of British history—we would be developing a collective memory and identity in which all can share equally, regardless of, and in addition to, any other cultural loyalties. There is no reason why such an approach should discredit or belittle non-national cultural ties. Collier stresses that Nyerere's schools did not educate children to think any less of their particular tribal heritage; rather, by providing an overarching national narrative, they allowed children to see their tribal or regional identities as part of a wider set of associations.

Many people will feel such an approach is more characteristic of America than of Britain; but then, if Collier's analysis is correct, there is a good reason why America, with its enormous ethnic and cultural diversity, has consistently sought to engender a sense of national consciousness and even pride through its public school system. If Britain is to emulate America's diversity (as seems to be the present policy), then we may need to adopt a more American approach to the dissemination of a shared public culture.

Finally, it is worth making the point that, for many pupils, some of the most important influences on their experiences outside of school are likely to be popular consumerist culture, peer pressure and, in some cases, gang membership. By weakening the substantive content of the school curriculum, the educational establishment has effectively privileged these forces over the enjoyment of cultural and intellectual goods which cannot be bought and sold, and which serve to enhance a child's mental independence. There is nothing 'progressive' or 'enlightened' about a policy which leaves children under the power of commercial influences. One of the objectives shared by thinkers as different from one another as Mill, Newman, Arnold and Antonio Gramsci, was that children must be educated to understand and resist the industrial and political forces ranged against them in modern society; by contrast many in the current educational establishment are proposing to make these forces the unexamined foundation of the school curriculum.

Conway's book opens the way to a new and more hopeful approach to education in Britain. A broad liberal education is the best means we have to ensure the development of our children as fully realised individuals—not only intellectually, but emotionally and aesthetically, in their character, conduct and self-image. By inviting each child to enter an imagined world which exceeds and leads beyond his or her pre-existing experience, a liberal education offers a liberation from the parochialism, materialism and estrangement of the modern world, and allows a child to experience life through the eyes of other cultures, epochs and worldviews. Moreover, by making a common cultural heritage available to all, it offers the means to harmonise and subsume into a wider relationship individuals and groups who might otherwise remain separate, isolated and mutually distrustful.

Justin Shaw
Chairman of Trustees, Civitas

Summary

1. How Schooling in England Went So Badly Wrong

The 1988 Education Reform Act imposed a legislative straitjacket on state schools in England that has denied their teachers and pupils alike scope for spontaneity and creativity.

It instated too much external testing on pupils, an overly bureaucratic regime of school inspections, and a too-closely-prescribed curriculum.

However, the William Tyndale affair a decade earlier had shown the need for greater regulation and monitoring of state schools.

The undoubted defects of the 1988 Act do not entirely vitiate the idea of a National Curriculum which continues to have prominent advocates in the field of education.

2. The National Curriculum as Culprit

In the form in which it was originally introduced, however, the National Curriculum commands ever-diminishing support among educationists. Many consider its subject-based character outmoded and unsuited to the needs of today's pupils.

It is said to favour in that form pupils of middle-class background, as well as to encourage disruptive behaviour among pupils alienated by its overly academic character.

In face of such criticisms, the National Curriculum is in process of being made ever less academic and subject-based.

Some have called for the National Curriculum to be scrapped in the interests of giving state-funded schools greater freedom to innovate and improve standards. Current Conservative Party policy appears to support exempting the new Swedish-style academies it favours from the constraints of a National Curriculum.

A supply-side revolution in state-funded schooling is possible without abandoning some form of National Curriculum for which there remains a strong case on grounds of social cohesion, as well as on purely educational grounds.

However, if the National Curriculum is to be retained, it needs to be made far less prescriptive than it presently is. Sweden offers a model of a less prescriptive national curriculum by which even its acclaimed academies are bound.

3. Some Common and Less Common Myths about the National Curriculum

Many critics of the National Curriculum claim it owes what they consider to be its unduly academic, subject-based form to its having been based upon the 1904 Board of Education Regulations for Secondary Schools in England.

They ground their claim upon the striking similarity between the subjects they both prescribe.

The subjects prescribed by the 1904 Regulations were those taught at that time in English grammar schools which the Board of Education wanted the new state-funded secondary schools to emulate.

One leading critic of the National Curriculum, John White, claims that the Edwardian grammar school curriculum itself derived from and was originally devised by England's Dissenting Academies. Their non-classical curriculum had been devised, he claims, to meet the religious preoccupations of their Puritan founders, and assumed its subject-based form through the influence upon Puritans of the sixteenth century French philosopher Petrus Ramus.

Whilst possibly suitable for those sharing the same other-worldly concerns as Puritans, White contends, that subject-based curriculum is unsuited to the this-worldly needs and interests of present-day schoolchildren.

4. On the Alleged Puritan Origins of the National Curriculum

Even were the origins of the National Curriculum to reside in the religious concerns of Puritans, such origins would no more necessarily discredit it than do the religious origins of Christmas make an annual festive season at this time of year unsuited to a secular age like ours.

The reason art and music were not taught at Dissenting Academies was not because their Puritan founders abhorred aesthetic enjoyment, but because their purpose was to train ministers, and, at the time they flourished, neither art nor music were included among the liberal arts considered suitable for teaching at places of higher learning.

Moreover, Ramus did not invent academic disciplines. Nor did Ramus devise his pedagogic method, or Puritans adopt it, so as to stifle free-thought, but to liberate thought from the incubus of the stifling form of scholasticism into the grip of which universities in England had fallen.

That Puritans opposed free-thought is a myth propounded after the Restoration and one to which John White seems to have fallen victim.

In any case, as shown in succeeding sections, the roots of the National Curriculum lie elsewhere than in the curriculum first devised and taught by England's Dissenting Academies.

5. The 1904 Regulations as the Alleged Source of the National Curriculum

The striking resemblance between the subjects prescribed by the 1904 Regulations and the National Curriculum does not prove the former to have been the source of the latter. The resemblance could just be due to coincidence.

Alternatively, the National Curriculum could have been derived from several other well-known prior publications which all propose similar curricula for English schools.

Some of these other prior publications antedate the 1904 Regulations by decades. If any prior works deserve to be considered the true source of the National Curriculum, it is these earlier works and not the 1904 Regulations.

6. The True Source of the National Curriculum

Several decades before the 1904 Regulations, Matthew Arnold had proposed a very similar curriculum for English secondary schools in two reports written in his capacity as a government inspector of elementary schools.

These reports were about the educational systems of France and Germany that had both instated such a curriculum in their secondary schools.

Arnold admired their systems and advocated England should follow their example by instating a similar national curriculum in its secondary schools that he argued should receive state subsidies as generous as those of their French and Prussian counterparts.

7. Liberal Education as the Purpose of the National Curriculum

The type of education Matthew Arnold envisaged was one he termed a *liberal* education.

It is just such a form of education that the National Curriculum sought to provide when it was introduced in 1988.

As conceived of by Arnold, liberal education proceeds in two stages: the first provided by schools; the second by universities. The goal of the first stage is to impart to students self-knowledge and knowledge of the world.

Self-knowledge—by which Arnold meant knowledge of human potentiality and capability—is inculcated through study of the arts or humanities; knowledge of the world through study of science.

Until only very recently, Arnold's view that the chief purpose of schooling should be provision of liberal education was widely shared by leading educationists in England.

Besides Arnold, other prominent English educationists who shared his view that liberal education should be the principal purpose of schooling include Robert Morant, H.A.L. Fisher, Cyril Norwood, George Sampson, and Michael Sadler.

They also include Lord Baker, chief architect of the 1988 Education Reform Act, although he never used the expression 'liberal education' when explaining the purpose of the curriculum introduced by that Act.

The logic of their position is scarcely even considered today by those critics of the National Curriculum who wish to see its originally prescribed set of subjects replaced by other, more vocational and socially 'relevant' forms of study and activity.

8. The Meaning, Origin and Rationale of Liberal Education

What was understood to be the meaning and purpose of a 'liberal education' by those who claimed its provision to be the principal purpose of schooling is little understood today. That incomprehension extends to leading educationists such as Richard Pring, director of the Nuffield Review of 16-18-year-old education.

Contrary to what Pring claims, the reason liberal education was distinguished from vocational education, and given that name, was not because it alone was considered to liberate its recipients from ignorance.

Rather, liberal education received its name, and was distinguished from vocational education, because its purpose and value were considered to be other than to prepare its recipients to earn their living.

The purpose and value of a liberal education were considered to lie in its enabling people to make good use of their leisure, possession of which is the distinguishing mark of free persons and the purpose for which they work.

The origins of liberal education go back to classical antiquity, specifically to Athens in the fifth and fourth centuries BCE. It was there that such non-vocational programmes of instruction were devised and provided to the sons of wealthy slave-owning Athenians.

Although they would never have to work for a living, such youth were thought to stand in need of special prior preparation so as to be able to make good use of the leisure that they would enjoy as adults.

The knowledge and skills that their instruction was designed to impart were such as, it was thought, would enable them to engage in effective political oratory, or else in philosophical enquiry and debate.

Such knowledge and skills became known as the 'liberal arts', such arts and knowledge as were considered to befit free men, in contra-distinction to the mechanical arts needed for purely vocational occupations.

Liberal education was adopted by the Romans and preserved by the Church during the Dark Ages, following the collapse of the Roman Empire. It was only with the return of more stable political conditions in the twelfth century that once again learning began to flourish in Europe.

That century saw the birth of universities in which liberal education was once again widely sought after and provided, albeit in the increasingly stylised, and eventually stultifying form known as schol-asticism.

Universities began to award bachelor and master of arts degrees to certify demonstrated levels of proficiency in the liberal arts. Such degree titles survive as legacies of that period, although now awarded as often for proficiency in vocational as in non-vocational subjects.

As understood by the likes of Matthew Arnold and Henry Newman, liberal education is as much about the cultivation of sensibility as about the cultivation of the intellect. Its receipt involves becoming acquainted with great literature as well as science, and so cannot be child-centred, since children cannot be expected to know without appropriate instruction what great literature and art is.

Like Henry Newman, John Stuart Mill was fully aware of the need for education to cultivate the sensibilities of students as well as their intellects, and that it could only do so by means of their exposure to suitable art and literature.

However, Mill also rightly saw that only families and local communities could moralise and socialise children, schools alone being unequal to the task.

Calls for a more vocationally oriented curriculum, if heeded, will reduce opportunities in school for study of the kind of literature that Mill and others maintained had a supremely edifying and ennobling effect upon students.

Some critics of the National Curriculum call for a more child-centred curriculum on the grounds that no imposed curriculum could command universal consent, but this claim ignores the extent of the consensus among scholars at any time as to what needs to be studied by all those seeking an education in their field.

Arnold considered the rightful purpose of education to be to acquaint students with the best that had been thought and said, equating such a corpus of art and literature with culture.

The purpose and value of disseminating culture in that sense of the term was always recognised by Arnold to be primarily practical, rather than just theoretical.

Without the widespread dissemination of culture, Arnold feared the conditions of modernity would brutalise sensibility and make for a more disorderly society. Those fears of Arnold have arguably been borne out by the huge increase in rates of criminality that have taken place in the last half century, especially among the young.

Crime has increased as marriage and religious observance have fallen into decline. Arnold recognised the usefulness of religious education as a moralising agent.

Liberal education was also valued by Arnold for its ability to provide the wherewithal to satisfy the need of humans to be able to find meaning and solace in a world that had become 'disenchanted' by the findings of modern science.

Contrary to the likes of present-day educationists like Richard Pring and Ivor Goodson, the solace and insight provided by culture was never considered by the likes of Matthew Arnold to be the special preserve of an elite.

Its provision to all can and should be the object of state-funded schooling, but that demands a curriculum of the sort advocated by Arnold and embodied in the subjects whose study was prescribed by the National Curriculum, when first introduced.

Provision by schools of culture is being threatened today by changes to the National Curriculum that have been championed by educationists who seem unaware of what the true purpose and value of such a form of curriculum was long understood to be.

9. Conclusion

While there is much wrong with state schooling in England today in consequence of the excessively constraining provisions of the 1988 Education Reform Act, the subjects whose study in schools it mandated do not form part of the problem.

Rather, state schools only need freeing from excessive testing, an overly bureaucratised regime of inspection, and excessively prescriptive programmes of study, to be able once again to make provision of liberal education their central purpose.

'In order to spend leisure in civilised pursuits, we require a certain amount of learning and education, and... these branches of learning and education and these subjects studied must have their own intrinsic purpose, as distinct from those necessary occupational subjects which are studied for reasons beyond themselves... Clearly then there is a form of education which we must provide for our sons, not as being useful or essential but as elevated and worthy of free men.' [1]

Aristotle

'Education is a training of the sensibility, an intellectual and an emotional discipline. In a society in which this discipline is neglected... one may expect any sort of religious, moral, social and political aberration, and eventual decomposition or petrification. And we seem to have little to hope from the official representatives of education.' [2]

T.S. Eliot

1

How Schooling in England
Went So Badly Wrong

'Hard cases make bad law': so runs an old legal adage. It is an adage that has seemingly been amply borne out by the dire state to which legislation designed to deal with one difficult case has reduced publicly maintained schools in England. To prevent the recurrence of the kind of riot that pupils at one small north London primary school were allowed to run in the early 1970s, all state schools for these last 20 years have been confined within a legislative straitjacket. It has denied teachers and pupils alike practically all scope for spontaneity and creativity. For the most part, England's state schools have been turned into joyless cramming factories whose teachers, when not valiantly struggling to preserve order, can do little more than prepare their pupils for the incessant battery of mindless tests that they now face throughout their schooling.

The law which came to impose this straitjacket on England's schools was the 1988 Education Reform Act, and the refractory school whose orchestrated descent into chaos occasioned its imposition was the William Tyndale School in the London Borough of Islington. More than a decade separates the notorious goings-on there and that Act designed to prevent their recurrence. But so disquieting was their public disclosure that the resultant shockwaves long continued to reverberate in the minds of politicians and policy-makers. This was partly because, soon after publication of a report detailing them, the newly appointed Prime Minister James Callaghan delivered a ground-breaking speech about education in which he called for major changes in state schooling, partly in light of what had just been revealed to have gone on at that school.

Callaghan made his famous speech at the opening of Ruskin College in Oxford. In it, he spoke of 'the unease felt by parents and others about... new informal methods of teaching which... are... dubious when... not in well-qualified hands'.[1] Then, in what could not at the time have failed to be instantaneously recognised as a clear allusion to what had gone on at William Tyndale, he had remarked: 'There is no

1

virtue in producing socially well-adjusted members of society who are unemployed because they do not have the skills... of basic literacy, basic numeracy, the understanding of how to live and work together, [and] respect for others...'

The chaos at William Tyndale to which the Prime Minister had been so clearly alluding began shortly after the arrival of a new head in January 1974. 'During the first term, he agreed to give [one teacher] a free rein in his own class, and [the teacher in question] responded in kind with his children... They watched television or played table-tennis at will; they disrupted the school routine... by coming into class early, staying late, ignoring break rules and wandering all over the building at will (they took to using the staff toilets). Children were attracted from other classes... Other teachers tried to... emulate his methods. To some teachers, though, and a growing number of parents, it began to seem as though there was neither order nor teaching in the school.'[2]

Despite the increasing disquiet of some parents and teachers, and despite the matter being brought to the attention of the Inner London Education Authority (ILEA), the authority nominally responsible for the school, no action was taken about it for the remainder of that school year. At the start of the following year, chaos at the school was to spread further with the arrival of a new pair of teachers both highly sympathetic to the ultra-progressive regime its head had instituted. 'A child-centred, free-choice approach was now the order of the day... [W]hat the staff called team-teaching ... became the rule... [T]he corridor and... classrooms with their doors open were available for the different activities the children were free to choose from... [C]hildren were often unsupervised... [A] room referred cynically to by the teachers as a BFR "broken furniture room"... was used to store the remains of the desks, chairs, and so on that had fallen victim to the children's rage.'[3]

Only towards the end of that second school year did anyone in authority feel able or impelled to take action. In June 1975, after several managers had in desperation turned to the press, the ILEA finally decided to mount a full school inspection, prior to convening a public enquiry to determine what had gone on there and deciding what action to take. In protest at its forthcoming inspection that the ILEA was perfectly empowered to conduct under the terms of the 1944 Education Act, the head of the school and the staff there sympathetic to his approach went on unofficial strike. They briefly opened nearby a rival school for pupils whose parents were prepared to send them to it. Despite their strike having largely vitiated its purpose, the school inspection duly went ahead, as did the public enquiry which began the following October under the chairmanship of Robin Auld QC. For its duration, the head and other teaching staff who had taken unofficial strike action were suspended on full pay. Responsibility for the day-to-day running of the school passed to an acting head of more conventional pedagogic persuasion.

When the results of the public enquiry were finally published in July 1976, few in authority who had been associated with the school escaped blame. On the strength of its findings, the ILEA charged all staff who had taken strike action with misconduct. Its head was additionally indicted for having allowed the school to deteriorate so badly. All these staff resigned shortly afterwards, as did the chairman of the ILEA schools sub-committee who also came in for heavy criticism in the Auld Report for having not acted sooner once the matter had been brought to his attention. Several other managers associated with the school also resigned on the strength of its findings. Over and above the failings of the individual personalities associated with the school, the Auld Report also identified a number of systemic faults that had made the whole affair possible in the first place. It stated: 'The [education] authority has no policy: (1) as to standards of attainment at which its primary schools should aim; (2) as to the aims and objectives of the primary education being provided in its schools...; (3) as to the methods of teaching to be adopted in its schools.'[4]

It was to these systemic failings that James Callaghan was adverting in his Ruskin College speech later that same month. The public enquiry revealed that what had prevented the ILEA from acting sooner were structural constraints that, in principle, bound every other local educational authority in the country in relation to the schools for which they were nominally responsible. As the Auld report was pointedly to ask: 'If a headmaster is convinced that a particular educational policy or method is right for his school, and the district inspector is equally convinced he is wrong, by what yardstick does the inspector judge and seek to advise the head that he is wrong?'[5] A book published in the wake of the Auld report formulated the general problem that had been identified: 'The main ingredients... could be found all over the country:

a staff with strong radical convictions, a weak head-teacher, a dithering inspectorate, worried parents and a local education authority that did not know what it wanted of its... schools. The mixture was common enough, but previously it had not been thought of as dangerously explosive.'[6]

It was in large measure to address that structural problem that the 1988 Education Reform Act had been enacted. Its provisions concerning the curriculum and testing may well have been far too prescriptive. Even so, that would still not show that there had not been need for some kind of national curriculum, as well as for some more rigorous system of monitoring of school performance than had previously been in operation.

In his Ruskin College speech, James Callaghan mentioned several other issues besides those raised by the William Tyndale affair. Equally prominent among his concerns was how ill-prepared for employment he claimed their formal education had left many school-leavers and university graduates. He reported receiving 'complaints from industry that new recruits from the schools sometimes do not have the basic tools to do the job that is required'. He also claimed too many university students were opting for the humanities rather than science and that, of those who had opted for science, too many had been choosing pure science rather than the more vocationally useful applied sciences, such as engineering and technology. At the root of the problem, he claimed, lay an excessively academic secondary school curriculum, too oriented towards the humanities and insufficiently oriented towards technology. Callaghan summed up his several concerns so:

> There is a challenge to us all... and... in education... to examine its priorities... [S]ome of the fields that need study... are the methods and aims of informal instruction; the strong case for [a] so-called 'core curriculum' of basic knowledge; next, what is the proper way of monitoring the use of resources in order to maintain a proper national standard of performance; ... the role of the inspectorate in relation to national standards... [and] the need to improve relations between industry and education... Another problem is the examination system... especially in relation to less-academic students staying at school, beyond the age of 16.[7]

Many of the issues touched on by Callaghan in his speech continue to remain at the top of the political agenda so far as education is concerned. While many of New Labour's policies have been rightly said to be the continuation of policies instituted by the previous Conservative administration, so far as education is concerned it would seem nearer the truth to say that many of the reforms that were instituted by the Thatcher government were ones for which James Callaghan had first signalled the need in his Ruskin College speech. Only the exigencies of the hour prevented his fledgling administration from implementing them. It was left to the ensuing Conservative administration to address the issues that had been raised.

Above all, there were two main changes for which Callaghan had called that it fell to the subsequent Conservative administration to implement through the provisions of the 1988 Education Reform Act. The first such change was the introduction of a National Curriculum to ensure that schools taught science and technology, as well as literacy and numeracy. The second change was the much closer monitoring of pupil performance in schools to ensure they were teaching what they had now become by law required to teach. The legal straitjacket placed upon England's state schools by the 1988 Act arose less from these two changes *per se* than the specific manner in which it went about making them. The National Curriculum was introduced in far too detailed and prescriptive a manner. Likewise, the system of monitoring school performance that it instituted went far beyond anything that had been truly called for. A new beefed-up school inspectorate was created whose prescribed mode of inspection was far too paper-driven and time-consuming for schools. Also, and above all, their pupils became subjected to far too much external testing.

Always bitterly resented and complained of by the teaching profession at the time, slowly the defects of the 1988 Education Reform Act are becoming ever more widely recognised. One by one, its excessively constraining provisions are in process of being relaxed or abandoned. That many of its provisions are currently unravelling is not necessarily, however, any cause for unqualified celebration. By no means all its provisions were objectionable and some, indeed, were arguably laudable. Among those of its provisions which arguably were laudable, one was its reminder to maintained schools of their continuing statutory obligation to provide religious education and a daily act of collective worship.[8] Another was its stipulation of which other subjects besides religious education all maintained schools had to teach to ensure their pupils received a broad and balanced education.

Merely to have imposed a National Curriculum in the form of such a set of prescribed subjects would not itself have been oppressive or objectionable. Nor would it have been either of these things had there been instituted a much less onerous system of monitoring school and pupil performance. This could have been done by instituting one that involved only the random sample testing of pupils, and a light-touch regime of school inspections without advanced notice, but with more numerous classroom observations and far less paperwork demanded of school heads and staff. Instead, the heavy-handed manner in which the 1988 Act instituted the National Curriculum and the monitoring of school performance was both onerous and ill-judged. Schools became obliged to teach the prescribed subjects according to highly detailed schemes of study. Levels of attainment in the core elements of the curriculum became subject to measurement by external tests administered to pupils at the ages of 7, 11, 14 and 16. Test results became published in the form of national school league tables carrying potentially highly adverse consequences for schools that came low down in them. Concern to avoid being placed in such a potentially hazardous position became a higher priority for many schools than providing their pupils with a stimulating education.

The result of the simultaneous introduction of such a detailed and heavily prescriptive curriculum and such an intensive testing regime has been to deprive schools of the freedom that their staff and pupils needed to thrive. The overly prescriptive manner in which the National Curriculum was instituted, together with the needlessly elaborate and intensive system of pupil-testing, have helped to create a general culture within state schools whereby their ensuring satisfactory results in these tests has become their over-riding priority. That obsession with assessment has similarly changed the general nature of pedagogy even at A-level.

Among the most deleterious effects of the excessively extensive system of external pupil assessment introduced by the 1988 Act has been the encouragement of 'teaching to the test'. This is the practice whereby schools attempt to boost the test scores of pupils by repeated advanced drilling.[9] An equally baneful effect of the testing regime is that many schools have confined their attention in the years immediately before tests at 11 and 14 to the core subjects on which pupils are to be tested. The other subjects that they should also have been teaching have been neglected.[10] A letter from a retired primary school head, published by a national newspaper in May 2009, showed what damage the tests had caused. Concerning the key-stage 2 tests administered to primary school pupils at the end of Year 6, she had written: 'Preparation for the tests starts in Year 5 and takes up much of Year 6 because teachers' and head-teachers' careers depend on the results. As a former head teacher of two inner-city schools, I found myself under pressure to restrict the curriculum almost entirely to maths and English to enhance our published results.'[11]

A no less damaging effect of the testing regime instituted by the 1988 Education Reform Act has been that it has led some schools to neglect their brightest pupils, since they could be assured of reaching the desired attainment targets. Instead, they have given excessive, if not quite exclusive, attention to their border-line pupils, so as to ensure that they met the relevant attainment targets and thereby secured for themselves a safe position in the league tables. As a result, the brightest pupils have often been neglected by their schools and left feeling bored.[12]

The various ways schools have set about boosting the test scores of their pupils have little lasting or genuinely beneficial effect on their attainment levels. This is attested by the practice that many secondary schools have since instituted of routinely re-testing new pupils during the first term. They are re-tested because their schools know how unreliable have been their test results at 11, which have often been artificially and temporarily inflated through prior preparation. Meanwhile, the current obsession of schools with securing good examination grades has been extended into the teaching of A-levels, with equally harmful effect upon lessons and work assignments. As was reported by one student who had just completed her A-levels in the summer of 2008: 'Every lessons of the past two years—in my chosen subjects of Biology, Physics, Chemistry, French and Philosophy—have been focused on examinations. The year is structured around the syllabus and past papers... The system allows many students to leave school with a hat full of As having never faced an intellectual challenge.'[13]

According to the former head of Curriculum and Qualifications Authority Ken Boston, a measure of how dysfunctional state schooling has become is indicated by the fact that:

> So many young people, after attending school for more than 10 years, are found to be poorly equipped for employment... These youngsters are not necessarily the underperformers and school dropouts—many of them have good GCSE results and come from schools at or near the top of the league tables. Yet employers find that, despite their formal qualifications, many young people are unable to communicate simply and well; they cannot work in teams; they lack initiative, enterprise and the capacity to foresee and resolve problems; they cannot plan a schedule or manage themselves; and they lack a thirst for continued learning and personal growth... This situation is not a figment of employers' imaginations. It is real and it is a crisis.[14]

According to Boston, at the root of the present-day crisis in state schooling in England lies the current testing regime imposed on schools by the 1988 Act, especially that which has been imposed on primary schools. He claims: 'the Key Stage tests ha[ve] sucked the oxygen from the classrooms of primary schools... In all but those primary schools principled enough to resist the pressure upon them, the primary school curriculum has become a dry husk. The teaching programme focuses on what is to be tested and on practising for the tests, because the future of the school... is dependent upon the results.'

What has not been responsible for the present-day crisis in state education, according to Boston, is what the National Curriculum has required schools to teach. He claimed: 'The creation, growth, maturation and possession of the skills required to succeed in employment and in adult life depend on good teaching of a broad and enriched curriculum at primary school... The present problem is not the result of inadequacies in the primary curriculum... [T]here is not much wrong with it and much to be said in its favour. The real problem is that teachers and schools aren't able to get on with teaching it.'[15]

Boston's exoneration of the National Curriculum has received endorsement by Sir Michael Wilshaw, head of the highly successful Mossbourne Community Academy in Hackney, north London, which replaced the failed Hackney Downs School. A member of the Labour Government's national panel of expert advisers, Sir Michael has deplored the current trend towards replacing the separate subjects which it prescribed in its original form with multi-disciplinary 'areas of learning'. This replacement was a principal recommendation of the Rose Review of the primary curriculum published at the end of April 2009.[16] A similar move to replace academic subjects with areas of learning is also being fostered at the secondary level through such developments as the introduction of a new diploma in humanities and social science for 14- to 19-year-olds.[17] Following his appointment to the Prince of Wales' Teaching Institute, Sir Michael commented on these curricular changes by saying: 'I have been teaching for 40 years and when I started there wasn't a National Curriculum... We spent years trying to design one because we thought that it was important that there should be a national consensus on a body of knowledge. That wasn't so long ago and we shouldn't start mucking about with it too much... Life-skills, healthy living, environmental studies are all very important... [but] we can get subjects to cooperate with each other ... without institutionalising it... My concern is that if we lump things together and make them organisationally too complex we lose that in-depth knowledge... It has to be about rigour at the end of the day.'[18]

That a National Curriculum should consist of traditional academic subjects rather than skills and life-style classes is also the view of Bernice McCabe, head of North London Collegiate School and director of the Prince's Teaching Institute (PTI). In a PTI report published in May 2009, Mrs McCabe declared that: 'subjects should have priority. They are interesting in their own right as well as providing the bank of knowledge required for significant non-superficial exploration of important topics like sustainable development and the applications of technology... I am aware that this is not a fashionable view. Look at how syllabus requirements have been reduced in all the mainstream subjects. How many topics have been dropped from school mathematics and chemistry? How many fewer texts—and fewer still whole texts—have to be studied in English and foreign languages? Ask any university admissions officer. Look at the number of remedial courses which universities are having to provide in order to bring their new students' level of knowledge up to that required for embarking in an honours degree.'[19]

By no means all educationists agree with Boston, Wilshaw and McCabe, as we shall now see.

2

The National Curriculum as Culprit

In being unwilling to consider the National Curriculum a major cause of what is wrong with state education in England today, Ken Boston, Sir William Wilshaw and Bernice McCabe are in something of a minority among educationists. Many consider it to be excessively academic, and claim its being such is principally responsible for current low attainment rates, high truancy rates and for much of the disruptive class-room behaviour that is so rife in many state schools in England today. According to these critics of the National Curriculum, the overly academic and subject-based form in which it was introduced has left many less academically-oriented schoolchildren frustrated and bored at school. As a result, they argue, such pupils become alienated and disruptive, and thereby impede the progress of the more academically able and inclined ones.

It has partly been to cater better for less academically oriented schoolchildren that of late there have been growing calls for the introduction of new vocational pathways for 14- to 19-year-olds. Their introduction is destined to have a considerable impact on more traditional forms of pedagogy within secondary schools. The entire system of assessment is currently undergoing radical overhaul so as to confer upon these new vocational pathways parity of esteem with the more traditional academic subjects. The new Diploma in Humanities and Social Science, currently under construction, is designed to stand alongside the more vocational diplomas to offer 14- to 19 year-olds a somewhat more academic pathway than those, but one that is less academic than traditional A-levels. In time, it could well come to displace traditional A-levels in humanities subjects. Its substitution of social concerns for more traditional academic subject-matter was one of the trends against which Bernice McCabe was inveighing.

In an endeavour to make schooling of greater interest and appeal to less academically inclined schoolchildren, several other changes have been or are about to be made to the National Curriculum. These are all steadily undermining its previously academic subject-based character. Citizenship education became part of the National Curriculum in 2000.

From September 2011, it will be joined by Personal, Social, Health and Economic Education (PSHE). Primary schoolchildren will then as a result be obliged to receive lessons on puberty, sex and 'how to form and maintain relationships'.[1] All these changes to the National Curriculum are progressively making it ever less academic. Whether they will improve education or worsen it is the question to which the present study seeks an answer.

Among the many prominent educationists who claim the National Curriculum to be excessively academic is Tim Brighouse. A former chief adviser for London schools, Brighouse has called its introduction in that form 'a major accident of history... [that has] ill served our curriculum thinking'.[2] Brighouse is not opposed to a national curriculum as such, recognising the state has a right to a say in what is taught in the schools that it funds. However, he argues that, in the form in which it was introduced, the National Curriculum was ill-conceived. He claims: 'The purpose, scale, framework and choices for inclusion in the curriculum were inappropriate, inheriting the traditions of a bygone age.' Among its principal defects, he claims, was its anachronistically academic character: 'Technology aside it was a repeat of the 1904 grammar school curriculum defined in terms of subjects known to the nineteenth-century universities (which no more than one per cent of students attended). The range of subjects falls hopelessly short of describing the shape of higher education today and there is increasing dismay in this sector about the appropriateness of the curriculum.'[3]

Another critic of the National Curriculum to claim it was introduced in an unduly academic and subject-based form is John White, emeritus professor of philosophy at London's Institute of Education. In a lecture delivered in 2007, White asserted: 'When the National Curriculum appeared in 1988, it... consisted of ten foundation subjects... But there was no account of what these subjects were for. Kenneth Baker seems just to have taken over a traditional view of what constituted a good school curriculum.'[4] White rejects that traditional view. He claims that: 'The academic, subject-based curriculum is a middle-class creation... whose *effect*, if not intention, has been to make it difficult for many children not from a middle-class background to adjust to a highly academic school culture [it creates].'[5] White denies there was any adequate rationale for the subject-based form in which National Curriculum was introduced. Its having been given that character, he

11

argues, has been one reason that schoolchildren from a working-class background so often find their schooling uncongenial. He concluded his 2007 lecture by remarking that: 'The idea that a good schooling revolves only round traditional subjects... may now be due for retirement... [T]ime is wasted... when a misplaced push for effective learning leads to so many young people literally not wanting to know.'[6]

Martin Johnson is our third critic of the National Curriculum who takes exception to its subject-based form. Johnson is acting general secretary of the Association of Teachers and Lecturers (ATL) and head of education policy and research there. He claims that it has been responsible for much of the disruptiveness and disaffection towards studying prevalent in so many state schools today. In a report published by his union in 2007, Johnson claimed that: '*all* our pupils are impoverished by the current offering... not... just low achievers. Attitudes to learning of the successful are just as problematic as the disengagement of the unsuccessful.'[7] Johnson points out that: 'most people are not intellectuals... and do not live their lives predominantly in the abstract... [But] throughout the world education systems are based on the considered superiority of the abstract over the real, of thought over action.'[8] He argues the reason schools have been made to teach an inappropriate curriculum is 'because mass education systems developed in the twentieth century copied the curriculum considered necessary for social elites: leisured classes who could afford and valued such attitudes. Britain is not alone in failing to think through what would be useful learning when presented with 11 years of compulsory education.'[9]

In his report, Johnson outlined an alternative curriculum that he claimed would better suit the interests and needs of present-day schoolchildren. It would do so, he argued, because it would accord a much higher priority than does the National Curriculum to the inculcation in them of useful skills rather than 'useless' academic knowledge. Among the various allegedly more useful skills Johnson would like to see schools focus on, in place of teaching traditional subjects, are: 'physical skills such as walking and digging'; 'communication skills... [such as] body language, negotiating, giving and receiving criticism, assertiveness, [and] empathy'; 'intrapersonal skills... such as... self-esteem'; plus an assortment of political skills which schoolchildren are said to need for active citizenship. Such skills

12

are said to include those in 'combining with others to pursue shared interests and reacting to power exercised by others'.

Johnson argues that schools should not only accord less priority to traditional academic skills, they should also accord less priority to imparting specific bodies of knowledge traditionally associated with the different academic subjects. He claims any centrally arrived at view of which bodies of knowledge to impart to schoolchildren merely reflects the cultural perspective and predilections of whoever makes that decision. Accordingly, he claims, any body of knowledge that is imparted by a subject-based National Curriculum risks arbitrarily imposing on schoolchildren the tastes and outlook of a privileged few that might not suit many of them as much as would their initiation into some alternative culture closer to that of their families. Johnson writes: 'what is often called "high culture"… in reality is closely related to the lifestyle of an upper class which asserts the right to define quality… The problem of how to select what today's youngsters need from the explosively expanding volume of knowledge cannot be solved by reference to any version of classical education thought appropriate for a privileged class now long since past.'[10]

The attempt to foist upon all schoolchildren the present centrally-decided, academically oriented, subject-based National Curriculum, argues Johnson, merely breeds their resentment. He writes: 'a national curriculum with an overloaded knowledge specification… appears to pupils as an imposition. The knowledge is external to them, and because it is not determined with them in mind it seems not to be for them.'[11] In its place, that which schoolchildren should study and be tested on, he argues, should be left to their teachers to decide, subject to general oversight of the local education authorities responsible for the schools in which they teach. He claims: 'The Government needs [these] curriculum… reforms because otherwise it cannot meet its goals for raising the achievement of the least successful learners. Neither can it meet its aspirations for a future workforce with the skills wanted by employers… Yes, our children need the essential literacy and numeracy skills, but those who struggle with them need a different kind of learning opportunity to acquire them.'[12]

Should Johnson's proposed educational reforms be adopted, what schools teach would be decided in much the same way as it was decided before the 1988 Education Reform Act. Once again, state schools would become vulnerable to the kinds of misguided enthusiasm to which the pupils at William Tyndale School had been. All that it would take would be for some equally 'progressive' local education authority to share similar ultra-progressive enthusiasms of staff at some or all of the schools under its authority. It was precisely to prevent such a possibility from recurring that the 1988 Education Reform Act was enacted.

It may well be that the National Curriculum it instituted was excessively prescriptive in terms of what it called upon schools to teach. It may also be that it subjected pupils at state schools to far too much external testing. However, neither fact, if facts they be, would obviate the need for some form of national curriculum, as well as some form of external monitoring of pupil performance, to ensure that schools were teaching it effectively. Despite the lamentable state to which the 1988 Education Reform Act may have reduced state schooling in England, before all its provisions are abandoned as ill-conceived and undesirable, it is worth recalling the systemic defects the William Tyndale affair had exposed. Something needed to be done to ensure that never again could state schools become as dysfunctional as William Tyndale had been allowed to become before any countervailing action was taken. The 1988 Act may have caused the pendulum to swing too far in the direction of central control and regulation. That does not mean that there was not, and does not remain, need for some form of National Curriculum and some greater monitoring of school performance than had previously prevailed.

It was precisely to address those systemic failings, plus to meet several additional concerns, that James Callaghan had voiced in his 1976 Ruskin College speech, that the 1988 Education Reform Act had been enacted. Kenneth Baker made that clear in an interview he gave shortly before the 1987 general election. Included in his party's election manifesto had been the undertaking that, if returned to power, it would introduce a national curriculum. In this interview, Baker stated that the idea for such a national core curriculum had been his, but he added it was one 'all the political parties have come to accept' in the few months since he first announced his intention to introduce one. Then, after referring to the just published memoirs of James Callaghan, Baker had turned to his interviewer and asked: 'Have you read the Callaghan book? He realised that changes had to be made.'[13]

14

The educational changes introduced by the 1988 Education Reform Act may well have been in excess of what was necessary or desirable. That they were excessive would not show that a national curriculum was not then needed and does not still remain so. All that it would show is the need for a less heavily prescriptive curriculum and for a less intrusive testing regime than those introduced by the 1988 Act. A national curriculum might need merely to stipulate which subjects schools should teach, and in the case of each of subject, what knowledge of them pupils are expected to have acquired by the end of each strategic key-stage, formulated in the most general of terms.

Since the mid-1990s, Sweden has operated with just such a national curriculum. All schools are required to teach it, even the state-funded 'free-schools' on which the British Conservative Party plans to model a new generation of academies free from local authority control. As in the case of its 'free-schools', Sweden's national curriculum could form a useful model on which to base a more liberating national curriculum:

> The national curriculum [i]s set out in a single document with three sections: Goals and guidelines, Timetables and Syllabuses... The document itself is only 10 pages in length. The content is made up of goals and guidelines, clearly and directly addressing the professionals in the school... The curriculum although concise is clear...

> The curriculum and syllabuses are connected to each other and... provide the foundation for teaching. The syllabuses are a concrete transformation of the goals in the curriculum... *How the goals are to be attained, namely choice of content and method, is determined by the teacher...*

> The syllabuses for the respective subjects... express through 'goals to strive towards' the orientation of teaching in the subject by formulating the knowledge to be attained. The 'goals to be attained' set out the minimum level of knowledge in the subjects that all pupils shall attain in Year 5 and Year 9. In addition, the syllabuses express... both the purpose and the nature of the subject.[14]

> *Goals to attain...* in the ninth year of school are the basis for assessing whether a pupil should receive the 'Pass' grade... The syllabuses... do not lay down ways of working, organisation or methods... [but] provide a framework within which the choice of materials and methods are to be locally determined.[15]

Since 2003, the Swedish national curriculum has grown in length to 17 pages, but it still remains a masterpiece of compression by comparison with its English counter-part. One of the goals towards which schools should strive is that 'all pupils... acquire good knowledge in school subjects and subject areas.'[16] The prescribed subjects in the Swedish national curriculum are remarkably similar to those prescribed by the English National Curriculum. In the 2009 document setting out the syllabuses for each, they are listed as: art; English; home and consumer studies; physical education and health; mathematics; modern languages (besides English); music; science studies: biology, physics and chemistry; social studies: geography, history, religion, civics; crafts; Swedish and technology.[17] What Sweden expects, and by and large succeeds in getting, its schoolchildren to have learned by the end of the period of compulsory education at 16 is remarkably in advance of what England expects and succeeds in getting its children to do by that age. In England, one in five children leaves school without a single GCSE pass at grade C or above.[18]

The current unpopularity of, and hostility towards, the excessively detailed Programmes of Study prescribed by England's National Curriculum have served there to discredit the very idea of such a curriculum, even in so minimally prescriptive a form as Sweden's. Some have even argued that a National Curriculum should be altogether abandoned in England, claiming that: 'It is not only too prescriptive, but also associated with a faulty testing regime that has not accurately measured attainment.'[19] In their view: 'So long as the rigour of external examinations is maintained, each school should be permitted to devise its own curriculum... We must search for a new balance between government and citizens that confines central authority to what it can do best, without presuming to run everything.'[20]

Arguably, it would not be wise to abandon a National Curriculum in England altogether. Nor would it be necessary to do so to improve the efficiency of its schools funded by the state or the quality of the education that they provide. There is no reason to suppose retention of one in some less prescriptive a form, such as Sweden's, would not be fully compatible with a 'less politicised, unforced and pluralistic system that can serve the interests of the poor more effectively than a state monopoly'.[21]

It may readily be granted to some of its critics who want the National Curriculum scrapped altogether that: 'serving the interests of children from the poorest background is the crucial moral test that any

16

policy must pass'.[22] It is by no means obvious, however, that the interests of such children would best be served by leaving the decision of what they are made to study to be determined entirely by parental choice from a range of schools which have been entirely unconstrained by any form of centrally prescribed curriculum. Not to have any form of national curriculum would leave the way open for another William Tyndale debacle. By no means all parents of pupils there were opposed to the ultra-permissive changes its head introduced upon joining the school in 1973. The Auld enquiry found that: 'The parents... appeared to be divided almost equally between supporters and critics...'[23] Such a large degree of parental support for the policies of a head who had reduced to chaos the school of which he was in charge suggests that parents cannot always be relied on to judge wisely on behalf of their children's interests, when it comes to their schooling. Moreover, since that time, Britain has become home to a large number of immigrants from countries whose traditions and values are widely dissimilar and sometimes at variance with its own. In the case of the children of such immigrant families, it would seem singularly ill-advised to leave the type of education they receive entirely to the discretion of the schools to which many of them would be likely to be sent, if schools could be eligible to receive state-funding without the constraints of a national curriculum.[24]

It is not just what has been found to be taught by some independent Deobandi schools in England that gives cause for concern here. Almost equally problematic is what other sorts of minority school might be prepared to teach, or to refrain from teaching, if unconstrained by any form of National Curriculum. Consider, for example, Steiner schools to whose receipt of state-funding as academies the shadow education secretary Michael Gove publicly gave support in July 2009, after visiting one such school in Somerset.[25] Of the school he visited, he remarked:

> They were delightful people and it seemed an absolutely fantastic school. Parents who might not have much money have their children there. It seems to me this is exactly the sort of school that should be supported... My principal aim is not to say Steiner... for all. There are lots of parents would want to provide a more traditional style of education. But if the Steiner... movement succeed in convincing and attracting more and more parents then all to the good.[26]

17

While in no way wishing to take issue with the Shadow Education Secretary on the personal merits of the staff and pupils of the Steiner school that he visited, there are many legitimate concerns that can be raised about what Steiner schools teach and refrain from teaching, given the anthroposophical outlook of their founder Rudolf Steiner that informs the curriculum of at least some of them. One index of such concern is the fact that, shortly after Stockholm University took over the Stockholm Institute for Education in January 2008, it decided to wind up a four-year Steiner-Waldorf teacher training programme jointly run by the Institute and the Rudolf Steiner College in Bromma. It did so after its teacher education committee judged that: 'Steiner science literature is "too much myth and too little fact".'[27] When it announced its decision, the university stated that: 'The courses did not encompass sufficient theory and a large part of the subject theory that is included is not founded on any scientific basis.'[28] According to the dean of the university's faculty of natural science which has responsibility for all the university's teacher training courses: 'The syllabus contains literature which conveys scientific inaccuracies that are worse than woolly: they are downright dangerous.'[29] Concerning the university's decision, the university's rector has stated that: 'The committee do not criticise the Waldorf pedagogy in itself, but the literature which does not meet the university's scientific standards.'[30]

Since 2002, Steiner-Waldorf education has received state-funding in Sweden that has over one hundred Steiner-Waldorf schools; these are said to be directly threatened by the university's decision. There are currently 24 Steiner schools in England.[31] One such school, the Steiner Academy Hereford, became a state-funded academy in September 2008, having opened 20 years earlier as a fee-paying independent school. When deliberating in 2004 as to whether to award the school academy status and the state-funding that goes with it, the then Department for Education and Skills commissioned a report from a group of academics based at the University of West of England in Bristol about Steiner Schools in England.[32] A co-author of the report was Glenys Woods, a research fellow in the Department of Education at the University of Gloucestershire and 'an Angelic Reiki healer'.[33] According to the Angelic Reiki official UK website:

> Angelic Reiki is a powerful hands-on healing method that works with the
> highest energies of the Angelic Realm to bring about healing and balance on all

18

levels to those receiving the healing energy... During an Angelic Reiki Healing treatment, the person doing Angelic Reiki is simply a bridge for the angelic healing energy to pass to the recipient. Angels are not restricted by time and space. Working together with Angels and Archangels... allows us to reach deeply into all areas which require rebalancing and healing. In multi-dimensional Angelic Reiki healing the recipient is lovingly supported to let go of physical and emotional and karmic imbalances as well as ancestral issues through all time and space. It is a blessing to give and receive these angelic healing treatments.[34]

The report noted that the 'Steiner curriculum for science is based upon Goethe's observational approach', immediately before recommending the 'Government to facilitate dis-application of Steiner schools from the requirements of the National Curriculum'.[35] This is a recommendation that the present Government has apparently been willing to adopt. It is also one to which the Shadow Education Secretary seems equally willing to accede, having publicly committed himself both to the idea of allowing Steiner schools to receive academy status as well as for academies to be exempt from the National Curriculum. In an exchange in the House of Commons with the Education Secretary Ed Balls in November 2007, Gove stated of his party that: 'We want to give academies the same freedom that independent schools have.'[36] According to Eugenie C. Scott from the American National Centre for Science Education:

> ... if schools follow Steiner's views on science, education will suffer. Steiner believed... science needs to 'go beyond' the empirical and consider vitalistic, unobservable forces, a perspective also common in twentieth-century New Age healing approaches. Anthroposophical medicine... claims that disease is caused only secondarily by malfunctions of chemistry and biology, and primarily by a disturbance of the 'vital essence.' Anatomy and physiology *a la* Steiner are unrecognizable by modern scientists: the heart does not pump blood; there are 12 senses ('touch, life, movement, equilibrium, warmth, smell,' etc.) corresponding to signs of the zodiac; there is a 'rhythmic' system that mediates between the 'nerve-sense' and 'metabolic-muscular' systems. Physics and chemistry are just as bad: the 'elements' are earth, air, fire, and water. The four 'kingdoms of nature' are mineral, plant, animal and man. Color is said to be the result of the conflict of light and darkness. Typical geological stages are Post-Atlantis, Atlantis, Mid-Lemuria, and Lemuria.

> Waldorf teachers are supposed to teach Steinerian evolution. In this view, species were specially created, rather than evolving from one another, and 'spiritual beings were the creators.' 'Let us start from the point that the gods, or

the divine spiritual beings, decided to create the world and man. For this we have a good authority in the first chapter of the first book of the Bible.'[37]

Scott was quoting from a Steiner school 'teacher's training manual' published in the UK. There is no suggestion that this manual is still being used, but the conception of science taught by Steiner schools is sufficiently eccentric to wonder why, given his stated concerns to improve science teaching in state schools, the Shadow Education Secretary is happy with the idea of Steiner academies being exempt from the constraints that would be brought to bear upon them by their being required to adhere to a suitably less prescriptive version of the National Curriculum similar to Sweden's.

That there could well be an overwhelming case for a national curriculum has long been recognised by many champions of a system of independent schools funded by state-supplied vouchers. Among such champions of voucher funding to voice support for the idea of a national curriculum are Alan Peacock and Jack Wiseman. They indicated their support in an early Hobart paper defending voucher-funded schooling. Peacock and Wiseman began there from the assumption that government has an 'obligation to ensure universal education up to some minimum'. They also accepted 'the necessary activities of government for this purpose... [include] such matters as the (very broad) specification of curricular requirements and perform-ance, standards, the certification of schools and perhaps of teachers'.[38] They then pointed out that government can discharge these obligations in a variety of different ways, 'ranging from the public provision of all education facilities to completely private but publicly regulated provision'. In other words, Peacock and Wiseman both accept there can be need for a broad national curriculum, despite their favouring a voucher system.

Edward G. West is another advocate of a system of independent schools financed by state vouchers who concurs that such a system is fully compatible with a national curriculum. He also acknowledges that, should a country undergo settlement by a large number of foreign immigrants markedly different in cultural outlook from that of its native inhabitants, it could well be expedient for it to institute a national curriculum for the sake of social cohesion. He writes: 'Vouchers... are normally thought usable only in schools that satisfy stated conditions the fulfilment of which is checked by inspection. These conditions could quite practicably be arranged so as to encourage whatever... the authorities desired... Common curricula could... be "engineered" through the voucher system if it was felt necessary.' [39]

What these several champions of voucher-funded schooling have all recognised is that nothing about such a mode of financing schools precludes having a centrally prescribed curriculum. Some of them also recognise that, in conditions of great diversity resulting from large-scale foreign immigration, a country might well have good reason to insist that all schools in receipt of vouchers must adhere to some centrally prescribed national curriculum. That, indeed, is what shall be assumed in the remainder of this study. In short, those who rightly want the extra competition between schools that a voucher system, or some equivalent, would create need not fear that the retention of a suitably drafted national curriculum must prevent schools from being able to innovate or adapt to local circumstance.

Of course, wherever there is a national curriculum, it remains open to political manipulation or to simply unwise inclusions and exclusions. However, the absence of a national curriculum equally leaves it open for schools, or groups of schools, to become subject to still greater political manipulation, and to even less wise inclusions and exclusions. The extent of apparent parental support for the misguided policies instituted at William Tyndale should certainly give pause for thought to anyone calling for an end to the National Curriculum in all its possible forms. So too should consideration of what the sponsors of some recent faith schools have been keen to have them teach, including what has apparently been allowed to pass for science teaching at Steiner schools in England.

In any case, like nuclear weapons, once invented national curricula cannot simply be wished away. Even were an incoming Conservative government to succeed in turning every state school into an academy and exempting all of them from the National Curriculum or just scrapping it, it would still remain open for an incoming government of a more *dirigiste* persuasion to reinstate a 'politically correct' national curriculum upon being returned to power and to demand academies comply with it. Given that possibility, it would seem preferable for an incoming Conservative administration concerned to raise educational standards and improve science teaching to retain the National Curriculum but make it less prescriptive, rather than jettison it altogether.

Even if the idea of a national curriculum were scrapped, the question would still remain as to what should be taught at school. Schools and parents would still need to decide whether the subjects that had been prescribed by the National Curriculum in its original form did or did not constitute the best possible curriculum. Quite apart from the overly prescriptive manner in which the 1988 Education Reform Act obliged schools to teach it, many critics of the National Curriculum claim it to be inappropriate in terms of what it included as well as what it omitted. How correct their view is on this matter is the issue to which we now turn.

3

Some Common and Less Common Myths about the National Curriculum

Many critics of the National Curriculum who object to its subject-based form claim this is owing to its having been derived from the 1904 Board of Education Regulations for Secondary Schools. They ground that claim upon its striking resemblance to the curriculum prescribed by those Regulations.

The 1904 Regulations applied to all secondary schools in England in receipt of central government grants or aid. When issued, the only secondary schools in receipt of such funding were certain grammar schools that had started to admit pupils funded from such sources. However, the Regulations were principally devised with a different category of school in mind, schools not then in existence. These were schools that the newly created local education authorities had been authorised to build by the 1902 Education Act using revenue raised upon the local rate. They had been authorised to build such schools whenever local voters had decided there were insufficient places at existing grammar schools for all local children capable of benefiting from one. The 1904 Regulations were designed to ensure the curricula of these new secondary schools would be similar to those of grammar schools, rather than to the more practical and vocationally oriented curricula of the higher-grade elementary and central schools. These latter schools had sprung up towards the end of the nineteenth century, after ever larger numbers of working-class and lower-middle-class parents became sufficiently well-off to afford to keep their children in full-time education beyond the statutory minimum school-leaving age of 12. At the turn of the century, a High Court ruling known as the 'Cockerton judgement' declared the public funding of such schools to be *ultra vires*. As a result, creation of a new system of secondary schooling had become necessary. Its eventual design was largely the brainchild of Robert Morant, the forceful and far-sighted permanent secretary of the Board of Education who had been the principal architect of the 1902 Education Act which had created both that Board and local education authorities.

In the eyes of many critics of the National Curriculum, much that is wrong with schooling today in England stems from its having been modelled upon the curriculum prescribed by the 1904 Regulations. They claim it has been because it was so modelled that state schools today teach a curriculum that is inappropriately academic and deeply unsuited to the needs of many, if not all, contemporary schoolchildren. One early critic of the National Curriculum to claim this is Richard Aldrich, an historian of education at London's Institute of Education. In an anthology about the National Curriculum published in 1988, Aldrich remarked:

> To an historian the most striking feature of the proposed national curriculum is that it is at least 83 years old... There is such a striking similarity between [it and the 1904 Board of Educations Regulations for Secondary Schools] that it appears that one was simply copied from the other... Thus in essence the proposed national curriculum... appears as a reassertion of the basic grammar school curriculum devised at the beginning of the twentieth century.[1]

On the basis of that posited origin, Aldrich claimed the National Curriculum was unduly academic and outmoded. He remarked:

> Though the 1904 Regulations prescribed a much broader curriculum than that which had existed in the nineteenth-century Public Schools... they effectively checked any tendencies to technical or vocational bias in the secondary schools... [Moreover] one of the most striking features of the consultation document is the fact that curriculum is prescribed in terms of subjects... Not only is no awareness shown of non-subject approaches, the very list of subjects virtually mirrors that of 1904. Have there been no additions to knowledge since that date? Are economics, business studies, commercial skills, social studies, health education, personal and social educational programmes, life skills programmes... and a host of others, to be squeezed into a mere 10 per cent of time?[2]

Richard Aldrich's former colleague, John White, is another critic of the National Curriculum to claim that what he concurs is its unduly subject-based form is due to its having been based on the 1904 Regulations. Writing in the same anthology as Aldrich, White recounts how, a week before the 1987 general election, he had received a telephone call inviting him to a meeting with one of Kenneth Baker's aides. He recounts being told: '"The Secretary of State wants to know how to go about introducing a national curriculum. Can you come to a meeting with us next Tuesday morning?"'[3] With evident relish, White relates how he had politely declined the invitation, excusing himself by explaining how, on the morning scheduled for the meeting, he had arranged to take his 'daughter's pet weasel to be spayed'.[4]

White explained that his purpose in recounting the anecdote had been two-fold. He had related it, first, to illustrate what poor political judgement the Secretary of State for Education had shown in having turned to him for curriculum advice. This was because, as he confessed, he had long privately considered himself to be the 'Hammer of the Right'. His second purpose for recounting the anecdote was to show how little fore-thought could have gone into the design of the National Curriculum, given the apparent haste with which it must have been drawn up. White remarked: 'The incident shows... that as late as... May 1987 the Secretary of State had not the slightest clue about how to set up a national curriculum. It all points to a rush job, from first to last.'[5]

White's anecdote certainly adds credence to the suggestion that Kenneth Baker may have turned to some prior source for guidance when deciding what to include in the National Curriculum. On the strength of its similarity with the curriculum prescribed by the 1904 Regulations, White agrees with Aldrich in supposing it had been to them that Baker must have turned. He writes: '[its] very close similarity [with] … the subjects prescribed [in 1904] for the newly introduced state secondary (later grammar) schools… gives every appearance of… having been lifted from what was originally traditional grammar school practice'. [6]

Ivor Goodson is yet another critic of the National Curriculum to claim that it suffers from an unduly academic character on account of being based on the 1904 Regulations. Goodson is a professor of learning theory at Brighton University's Education Research Centre. In the form originally introduced, argues Goodson, the National Curriculum has been what he calls 'exclusionary', meaning it has condemned children from working-class backgrounds to educational failure. His contention is that it has done so by obliging them to study academic subjects that are of little relevance and so hold little appeal. By demanding they study such subjects, he claims the National Curriculum has doomed to failure New Labour's efforts to increase social inclusion and upward mobility through education. This is because it has obliged children from working-class backgrounds to study subjects of little appeal, and in which, as a result, they are bound to do badly. Goodson contrasts those subjects with several others that he claims are of greater appeal to such pupils and which he further claims were in process of being introduced into comprehensive schools when the National Curriculum put an abrupt stop to their introduction. Those allegedly more congenial subjects are said to be environmental studies, community studies, urban studies, women's studies and social studies. All these subjects, claims Goodson, had been developed by other 'vocational and pedagogic traditions [more] likely to promote social inclusion'.[7] The 1988 Education Reform Act abruptly ended the attempt of comprehensive schools to introduce that more inclusive curriculum, he argues.

Like Aldrich and White, Goodson claims that the more exclusionary curriculum instated in 1988 had its origins in the 1904 Regulations. He writes: 'The dominance of academic subjects goes back to the battle over which subjects should be prioritised in the new secondary schools at the start of the twentieth century. Morant's Secondary Regulations handed victory to the public-cum-grammar school vision of education and school subjects... This pattern of social prioritising was finally consolidated in the new "National Curriculum" of 1988 which almost exactly re-established Morant's Secondary Regulations of 1904—the Public School Grammar School Curriculum was firmly reinstated.'[8]

Goodson claims that the introduction of a curriculum so ill-suited to children from working-class backgrounds was not accidental. He writes: 'School subjects, it seems, have to develop a form acceptable to the "higher orders" of society... whose very position depends on social exclusion.'[9] He claims it was their prescribed study which accounts for why, despite the best efforts of New Labour to promote social inclusion through education, it has failed to increase the university participation rate of students from families without any previous history of university attendance. Its efforts were always doomed to fail, he claims, because of the uncongenial nature of the subjects the National Curriculum had obliged such schoolchildren to study. 'New Labour... never... questioned the exclusionary foundations on which their policies were to be built... They pursued social inclusion employing a wide range of well-honed exclusionary devices... The results were... precisely... further extended social exclusion.'[10]

The view that the National Curriculum was based upon the 1904 Secondary School Regulations seems now to have become very well-entrenched among those of its critics who claim it is unduly academic and subject-based. It was reiterated, for example, in December 2008 in a Working Paper for the Nuffield Review of 14-19 Education and Training. The author of this paper, Mark Hewlett, asserted in it that:

> In searching for a more relevant, dynamic, intellectually challenging, coherent, aims-led approach than we have experienced under the standard curricula of GCSE/National Curriculum and A-level, the very last thing I would want to do is encourage anyone to simply reach uncritically for something "off-the-shelf", as teachers in schools have done for over a century in accepting and implementing a subject-based curriculum, modified from what was considered appropriate for grammar schools boys in 1902, now quite inappropriate to meet the needs of students and government in 2008.[11]

In sum, much that is wrong with state education today is held by critics of the National Curriculum to result from its having been based upon the 1904 Regulations whose own prescribed curriculum was devised to ensure the curriculum of state-funded secondary schools would be like those of the grammar schools of that period. But whence did that grammar school curriculum originate, and what was its original rationale? Was it intended to be exclusionary, as Goodson claims it was? If not, exactly what were its origins and rationale? John White has recently proffered answers to these questions.

White has not been content with claiming the National Curriculum to have been modelled upon the curriculum prescribed by the 1904 Regulations and that curriculum modelled on the curriculum of Edwardian grammar schools. Lately he has imputed to that grammar school curriculum a certain origin and original rationale. It is one which he claims explains why the National Curriculum is so singularly ill-suited to present times. He claims that the Edwardian grammar school curriculum had originally been devised and taught at the Dissenting Academies that flourished in England during the eighteenth century. These Academies had sprung up after non-conformists had been prohibited by the earlier Test and Corporation Acts from being able to attend or teach at English grammar schools and universities. In 1769, after non-conformists became able to teach at grammar schools, White claims that they started to do so in increasing number. With them, he claims they brought the more modern curriculum with which they had become familiar by having attended and taught at Dissenting Academies. This more modern curriculum, he claims, increasingly came to displace the classical curriculum previously taught at English grammar schools for centuries.

Including, as it did, science, modern languages, mathematics and English, the Dissenting Academy curriculum was considerably more modern and 'realistic' than the classical one it came to displace in English grammar schools. However, White argues, it was still unduly narrow and inimical to free-thought. This was, he claims, on account of the religious purpose of personal salvation for which it had been devised. White claims:

> Knowledge of God's world was crucial in the dissenting thought world as a necessary condition of personal salvation[12]... The world of the Old English Dissenters and Scottish Presbyterians... was a world where personal salvation was thought to depend on having a comprehensive grasp of the nature of God's world.[13]

For a school curriculum to have such a religious purpose as salvation does not in itself entail that it must necessarily be unduly narrow or constraining of free-thought. However, White further argues that the Dissenting Academy curriculum was bound to be these things on account of the Puritan backgrounds of those who established these Academies and devised their curricula. He writes: 'Art... had little or no place in the academies, their emphasis being on knowledge. Imagination and emotion... were thought of ... as tempters to error.'[14] Still worse, he argues, because of certain religious preconceptions of those who devised their curricula, the knowledge that Academies came to impart was taught in hermetically sealed subjects whose rigid separation from each other, he claims, did little to encourage students to think for themselves.

White traces the origin of the thought-constraining character of the curriculum of the Dissenting Academies to what he claims to have been the baneful influence exerted upon Puritan educational thought by the novel system of pedagogy that was devised and propounded by the sixteenth-century French philosopher Petrus Ramus. Ramus was a convert to Calvinism and among the French Huguenots slaughtered in the St Bartholomew's Day Massacre in 1562. Thereupon, in the eyes of Protestants throughout northern Europe, he assumed martyrdom status, and his pedagogic system became highly esteemed among them.

Ramus had devised his pedagogic system to facilitate the transmission of knowledge in what he considered to be the most logical order possible. He considered knowledge to be best imparted in accordance with three laws of thought he claimed to have discovered in the writings of Aristotle. The first such law required the exclusion from the teaching of any art or science of everything not strictly relevant to it. Each art and science was considered to have its own unique subject matter. The second law required the exclusion of every proposition less than universal and necessarily true. Teaching any science or art required the elimination of all local and contingent information. The third law demanded that the teaching of every science and art had to proceed from the most abstract and general categories and concepts to the most particular and concrete ones.

White claims it was the adoption within Puritan circles of Ramus' pedagogic method that was responsible for the Dissenting Academy curriculum having come to assume its rigidly subject-based, thought-denying form. He observes:

> It is easy to understand the attractiveness of the Ramist method to Puritan or allied sect preachers, schoolmasters and textbook writers in the late sixteenth and early seventeenth centuries... given their interest in transmitting to their audiences huge quantities of orthodox information *rather than encouraging them to think for themselves*... Puritans used Ramist logic not to promote free thought but to show the one true path that understanding must take... They sought 'not man's intellectual domination in a rational universe, but rather a subordination of human reason to the demands of an enthusiastic faith.' [15]

After non-conformists began to teach at English grammar schools, they brought this rigidly subject-based thought-constraining curriculum with them. It was as the curriculum of these schools that it became prescribed by the 1904 Regulations which in turn served as the source of the 1988 National Curriculum. Hence, claims White, it has ultimately been its Puritan origins which account for the unsuitable subject-based academic form of the present National Curriculum. He remarks:

> With the priority it gives to more abstract subjects... and its insistence on sharp, non-over-lapping divisions between branches of knowledge... [Ramus's logic] has more than faint echoes...in the traditional school subject-based curriculum we know today.

> What had grown up in the eighteenth century as a curriculum suited to the religious beliefs of the minority community of Old Dissenters has become, three

centuries later and through various transformations, the taken-for-granted curriculum of the whole nation.[16]

Such a school curriculum might once have been suitable for the hide-bound Puritans who devised it. However, such a curriculum is deeply unsuited to the needs and interests of present-day school-children, contends White. Their schooling, he argues, should be aimed at encouraging their autonomous thought and their aesthetic enjoyment of the world. Such purposes, he claims, are ones the Puritans shunned. Thus, White concludes his article on 'The Puritan origins of the 1988 school curriculum in England' by remarking:

> For two and a half centuries the academic subject-based curriculum had a clear rationale. A comprehensive understanding of the myriad features of God's created world, coherently marshalled under discrete, non-overlapping subjects was seen as a necessary condition for one's own salvation. This justification has long since crumbled away and no compelling alternative has taken its place... It is not too optimistic, perhaps, to hope that sometime in the twenty-first century our eighteenth century curriculum may no longer have a future.[17]

Under the combined weight of such attacks against the National Curriculum as those levelled at it by critics such as Aldrich, White and Goodson, small wonder is it that confidence in the suitability of the traditional subject-based form in which it was introduced has begun to crumble. As the claims of such critics about its origins, social function, and original rationale have gained ever wider acceptance, so has the National Curriculum started to undergo revision. Its traditional academic character is steadily giving way to a new, different type of school curriculum. It is one more concerned to promote social adjustment, according to the values associated with a distinct political outlook, than with traditional pedagogic concerns.

If what these critics claim about the origins and rationale of the National Curriculum is correct, perhaps, these recent revisions to it may have been no bad thing. In the course of the nineteenth century, the traditional preoccupation of English grammar and public schools with the classics was rightly made to give way to a more modern curriculum. For the first time, these schools began to teach English language and literature, modern European languages and natural science. In the same way, the curriculum which they then began to teach, and which the National Curriculum replicated when introduced, might today rightly be undergoing similar replacement by one more relevant and better suited to contemporary circumstances.

Or, again, perhaps it might not. Suppose that the true origin and rationale of the National Curriculum is completely different from what its critics claim it to have been. Suppose that its true origins and rationale confer upon it in the form in which it was introduced a much more abiding relevance and suitability than its critics claim it to have had. Then, many or most of the revisions it has lately undergone and is continuing to undergo could all be for the worse. It is to determine whether these changes to the National Curriculum have been for the better or for the worse that we now turn to consider how correct are the accounts its critics have given of its origins and rationale. We start with John White's claim that, in the form in which it was introduced in 1988, the National Curriculum was tainted by what he claims to have been its Puritan origins.

4

On the Alleged Puritan Origins of the National Curriculum

John White contends that, in the outmoded form in which it was introduced, the National Curriculum has its origins in the narrow-minded religious concerns of the Puritans who devised the Dissenting Academy curriculum on which it was ultimately modelled. Even should White be correct in claiming the National Curriculum to have had Puritan origins, such origins would not automatically establish its subject-based form as outmoded or unsuitable to a secular age such as ours. The annual festivities of Christmas have ultimately religious origins, although, arguably, these are as much pagan as Christian. Such origins do not nullify the value of such annual festivities in so secular an age as ours. In any case, White seriously mischaracterises the nature of Puritan educational concerns in such a way as to place them in an unduly negative light.

In the first place, contrary to what White claims, the reason why art was not taught at Dissenting Academies was not because their Puritans founders abhorred aesthetic enjoyment, viewing the emotions as possible sources of temptation. This is so for several reasons. First, the reason Academies were initially set up was to provide the equivalent of a university education to those whom the Tests Acts had excluded from English universities. At that time, fine art was taught at neither Oxford nor Cambridge, nor at any other universities in Europe. The reason why art was not then taught at university, and hence the reason it was not made part of the Dissenting Academy curriculum, had nothing to do with religion in general, let alone Puritanism in particular.

From classical antiquity onwards, neither painting nor sculpture was considered a liberal art, and so worthy of being taught at universities or grammar schools. That remained the prevailing view well into the early modern period, as was noted by the historian of education Foster Watson. He writes: 'appreciation of the educational value of drawing and sculpture did not penetrate into the educational practice of the period. It is doubtful whether any instance can be produced of the actual inclusion of drawing in the curriculum of a grammar school in the Tudor period.'[1] While the far-sighted eighteenth-century Scottish educationist George Turnbull did call for the inclusion of fine art within the school curriculum, 'he stood virtually alone in his enthusiasm for art.'[2] Given that Dissenting Academies sought to provide the equivalent of a university-level education at a time when fine art was not taught at them for reasons that had nothing to do with religion, it hardly seems right to claim peculiarities in the religious sensibility of the founders of these Academies to be the reason art was not taught at them, as White does.

Second, even had some universities begun to teach art during the period in which Dissenting Academies flourished, their not having done so could still not correctly be attributed to any theologically-grounded fears that their founders and patrons might have had about the emotions and the imagination which is why White claims art was not included in their curricula. The primary purpose for which such Academies were established was to serve as seminaries for the training of future preachers, although other students were admitted. Given that was their primary purpose, it would have been no more appropriate for these Academies to have taught fine art than it would have been for artists' studios to teach their apprentices divinity.

Third, the reason art was not taught at Dissenting Academies could not have been, as White maintains, because their Puritan founders mistrusted the emotions and the imagination. This is because Puritans harboured no such mistrust. As has been pointed out about them: 'Puritans... were not... hostile to the arts themselves. Puritans associated art in churches with Catholicism, but they bought art for their homes. They objected to theatres, which had become centres of prostitution and dissipation in their day, but they did not necessarily object to dramatic art... for private performance. Oliver Cromwell owned an organ, and he hired an orchestra and had held dancing at his daughter's wedding.'[3]

White's account of the influence of Puritan concerns upon the curriculum of Dissenting Academies suffers from a still deeper flaw. He claims Puritans took an early keen interest in the emerging natural sciences and in the teaching of them because they believed scientific knowledge was needed for personal salvation. However, Puritans harboured no such belief. It is true that they did take a strikingly keen early interest in the 'new learning', being among its principal and most enthusiastic early supporters in England. For example: 'Among the group of ten scientists who during the Commonwealth formed the nucleus of the body that was to become the Royal Society, seven were strongly Puritan. Sixty-two per cent of the members of the Royal Society in 1663 were clearly Puritan by origin... [when] Puritans constituted a minority of the population.'[4] Moreover, it is true that their early interest in science was inspired by their religious faith. However, there is no historical warrant for supposing that the early interest they took in science stemmed from a belief that knowledge of it was needed for salvation, as White claims was their reason. As the Dutch historian of science Reijer Hooykaas has noted: 'What strikes one most about the early Protestant scientists is their love for nature in which they recognise the work of God's hands and their pleasure in investigating natural phenomena... The duty of scientific education was not regarded as an oppressive law, but rather was enjoyed as a duty of love and gratitude.'[5]

White makes a further claim about the pedagogy of Puritans that is no less tendentious than is his claim that their interest in science stemmed from their belief in the need of knowledge of it for salvation. He claims that Puritans adopted the Ramist pedagogic method because its separation of knowledge into discrete subjects served to stifle free-thought and this was something that they wanted to do. There are several things wrong with this explanation of why the Dissenting Academies' curriculum assumed the subject-based form that it did. In the first place, Ramus devised his pedagogic method for the systematic teaching of subjects, the individuation of which into separate arts and sciences had occurred centuries, if not millennia, earlier. He devised his method to facilitate their teaching and learning; not to bring them into existence. As has been noted by the Renaissance scholar Paul Oskar Kristeller: 'Ramus... largely followed the old scheme of the liberal arts and the university curriculum of... [his] time.'[6]

Second, contrary to what White claims, there is no evidence that the reason Puritan educators adopted the pedagogic method devised by Ramus was in order to prevent their students thinking for themselves and to subordinate their reason to the demands of an enthusiastic faith. Puritan educators adopted the method of pedagogy devised by Ramus for no different a reason than that for which he had devised it. This was an entirely opposite reason to that White claims. Ramus devised his method, and Puritan educators came to adopt it, because it liberated thought from the incubus of ancient authorities such as Aristotle, as those authorities had come to be accepted by scholastic thought. It has been justly observed of Ramus that his: 'most fundamental contribution... was his aid to the emancipation of society from medieval authority, and to the enfranchisement of truth and free investigation. Through him were secured some latitude in the field of knowledge and freedom from the ecclesiastical domination of reason... [He] freed the human spirit from the dungeon of Aristotle, and drew it forth from the medieval twilight. He improved all the literary and expression studies, and helped give mathematics and science a start'.[7]

Puritan educators adopted Ramus' pedagogic method for no different reason than that for which he devised it. Nor was it utilised by Dissenting Academies for any different reason. In claiming that Puritans adopted Ramus' pedagogic method to constrain free-thought and subordinate reason to faith, White seems to have relied upon a study of Puritan education by John Morgan.[8] It is from the conclusion of that work that White is quoting when he asserts that: 'the intentions of Puritan educationalists ... were far from embracing the new Enlightenment world that was beginning to emerge. They sought "not man's intellectual dominion in a rational universe, but rather a subordination of human reason to the demands of an enthusiastic faith".'[9] It is difficult, however, to see on what basis Puritan educators can justly be accused of having wanted to *subordinate* human reason to the demands of an enthusiastic faith. Nowhere is there in Morgan's book any reference to or discussion of Reijer Hooykaas' classic study *Religion and the Rise of Modern Science,* suggesting that Morgan may not have been aware of it. In his book, Hooykaas provides a very convincing explanation of how and why Puritans came to acquire what he shows to have been a largely unjustified reputation for having been opposed to free-thought and been willing to subordinate reason to the demands of an enthusiastic faith. Assuming it is correct, his explanation of their acquisition of that false reputation entirely subverts the basis for White's claims about the motivations of Puritan educators.

According to Hooykaas, after the Restoration, conservative-minded Anglicans began to attack Puritanism. They began to claim that Puritanism, the earlier political dissidence, and the new learning had all been apiece. After the Test Acts were imposed, a split occurred among

Puritans between those who were willing to conform to the articles of the Anglican creed and those who were not. The latter, in consequence, thereafter acquired the names of 'Dissenters' and 'Non-Conformists'. Hooykaas claims that, to deflect from themselves the attacks of these conservative-minded Anglicans, the Puritans who had conformed began to dissociate themselves from those Puritans who had chosen not to. The former began to blame the latter for all the excesses of the former Commonwealth period. At the same time, in order to safeguard the new science against being judged guilty by association with former political dissidence, its supporters began to portray the non-conforming Puritans as having been opposed to it as well as given over to religious enthusiasm. They did this by portraying them as being doctrinally similar to other more radical sects, such as ultra-spiritualists and Anabaptist millenarians, of whom some had opposed the new learning and been given over to religious enthusiasm. Hooykaas sums up the situation so: 'After the Restoration... since Puritanism was in disgrace but the new Philosophy was now under royal patronage, the *defenders* of the new science now deemed it expedient to deny any connection with Puritanism by identifying the latter with those "enthusiasts" who disliked learning.'[10] It was through that unwarranted association, he claims, that non-conforming Puritans acquired the reputation for opposing the new learning, as well as being willing to subordinate reason to an enthusiastic faith. In the vast majority of cases, he points out, that reputation was unwarranted.

All that the majority of non-conforming Puritans had ever contended was that a university education was not necessary to qualify someone for ministry or preaching. All they considered to be needed for this task, besides faith, was an intimate knowledge of Scripture. Such a conviction can hardly be said to amount to willingness to subordinate reason to faith. Quite the opposite is the case, given how abysmally poor in quality was the largely scholastic education still provided at the time by England's only two universities. Because of their perfectly justified repudiation of it, and because of their unjust alignment with other sects given over to religious enthusiasm, after the Restoration a legend came to be born that Puritans had been enemies of the new learning and willing to subordinate reason to the demands of an enthusiastic faith. The facts, however, tell a different story. Hooykaas points out: 'In general, the natural sciences, so seriously neglected in the universities, were positively appreciated. Even those political extremists, Gerrard Winstanley the Digger and William Walwyn the Leveller, wanted a reform of education that would give their due place to science and its applications... Again the Quakers in England, after the second half of the seventeenth century, took an active interest in applied science.'[11]

Suppose, however, that Puritans had been the close-minded religious enthusiasts whom White claims them to have been. Had they been, this fact might lend some weight to his claim and that of other critics of the National Curriculum that it lacks present-day suitability. But it would do so, only if White were also correct that the origins and ultimate rationale of the National Curriculum reside in Puritan religious concerns. However, as we shall now see, there is no reason to impute its subject-based character to the influence that the curricula of Dissenting Academies may have had upon those of early Edwardian grammar schools. There is better reason to ascribe to the National Curriculum an altogether different aetiology from that which White ascribes to it. This alternative aetiology provides it with an entirely different rationale from that which White claims was its original one. It is a rationale that confers upon the National Curriculum a far more abiding relevance than does White's posited one.

5

The 1904 Regulations as Alleged
Source of the National Curriculum

As mentioned previously, critics of the National Curriculum who take exception to its subject-based form often claim it is due to its having been derived from the 1904 Regulations for Secondary Schools. They base that claim upon its striking resemblance to the curriculum that was prescribed by those Regulations. However, their mutual resemblance does not by itself establish that the later curriculum was based upon the earlier one. There are several other possible ways to account for their mutual similarity. One way is to ascribe it to sheer coincidence. That the resemblance was the result of coincidence is not without some evidence.

In all the several accounts he has ever given as to how and why the National Curriculum came to assume its original form, nowhere has Kenneth Baker ever mentioned the 1904 Regulations as having been a source of inspiration for it. Rather, he has only dwelt on the intrinsic merits of the several subjects it prescribed. Consider, for example, what Baker writes in his political memoirs about the discussions he had at the time with the Prime Minister on what the National Curriculum should contain. These discussions occurred shortly after he announced his intention to introduce a national curriculum shortly after becoming appointed Secretary of State for Education, but before it had been decided what it should contain. In those discussions, Baker recounts: 'the Prime Minister warned against over-elaboration of the Curriculum and said that she wanted to concentrate on the core subjects of English, maths and science.'[1] By contrast, he explains, he had supported a broader curriculum. He writes: 'In the debates that took place before and after the Election this proved to be the central issue. I believed that if we were to concentrate just upon the core subjects then schools would teach only them and give much less prominence to the broader range which I felt was necessary.'[2] He then adds:

> I wanted to ensure that every boy and girl took not just science but also technology… Furthermore, I wanted to ensure that not only was the teaching of [foreign] languages more relevant and practical but that all children had to

continue with them up to sixteen. I also wanted to ensure that as regards history children would leave school with real knowledge of what has happened in our country over the last 1,000 years... Geography too was important but ... in danger of disappearing into the less rigorous form of environmental studies... I also wanted to include art, music and sport.[3]

Such a piecemeal explanation as Baker gives here for why the National Curriculum eventually came to include the subjects it did does not read as that of someone who had turned for guidance as to what to include in it to some earlier source. Admittedly, had he done so, Baker might well not have wanted that fact to be widely known. However, if he had turned for guidance to some earlier source when deliberating about what to include within the National Curriculum, its mere similarity to the curriculum prescribed by the 1904 Regulations does not establish that it had been to those Regulations he had turned. Similar curricula had been proposed in several other prior works. It might just as easily have been to one of them that Baker turned for guidance, had indeed he turned to any prior works at all.

One alternative possible source from which Baker might have derived the National Curriculum is the 1927 'Hadow Report' *The Education of the Adolescent*. Colloquially named after Sir William Hadow, chairman of the Board of Education committee that produced it, this report proposed a curriculum for the junior years of all secondary schools in England no less similar to the National Curriculum than that prescribed by the 1904 Regulations. A second possible source from which Baker might have derived the National Curriculum is the 1943 'Norwood' Report *Curriculum and Examination in Secondary Schools*. Named after Cyril Norwood, chairman of the committee that produced it, this report also proposed a common curriculum for the junior years of all secondary schools in England no less similar to the National Curriculum than is that prescribed by the 1904 Regulations. It could, therefore, just as easily have been from where Baker had received guidance on what to include within the National Curriculum, assuming he had sought guidance from some prior work. There is yet a third possibility. In 1909, three decades before the 1943 report which bears his name, Cyril Norwood had been co-author of a book about secondary education in which a curriculum had been proposed for the junior years of all secondary schools in England that is no less similar to the National Curriculum than is that prescribed by the 1904 Regulations.[4] Based purely upon considerations of similarity and historical priority, therefore, it might have been from it that Baker had derived the National Curriculum.

In the absence of some special reasons for supposing the 1904 Regulations to have been the source of the National Curriculum, therefore, there is no reason to suppose that they were. It might be thought their historical priority to the three other works mentioned in which similar curricula are proposed constitutes that special reason. For even had it been from one of them that Baker had derived the National Curriculum, their proposed curricula could conceivably have been inspired by the 1904 Regulations. However, even should their historical priority to these three other works give those Regulations a better claim to be considered the source of the National Curriculum, it would not give them the best claim. For the 1904 Regulations are not the earliest document in which a curriculum is proposed for English schools similar to the National Curriculum in those ways its critics find so objectionable. Several decades before the turn of the nineteenth century, two works had proposed for schools in England a curriculum almost as similar to the National Curriculum as that prescribed by the 1904 Regulations.

Moreover, the view of education espoused by these two earlier works is one the 1938 Spens Report on Secondary Education claimed was 'the basic idea underlying the Prefatory Memorandum and the Regulations of 1904 so far as they deal with curriculum'.[5] Further still, Cyril Norwood quoted extensively from one of these two works in that section of his own 1909 book in which a curriculum was proposed for secondary schools in England very similar to that prescribed by the 1904 Regulations. This suggests that this prior work is also likely to have influenced whoever drew up the 1904 Regulations. Therefore, even had Baker turned for guidance on what to include in the National Curriculum to the 1904 Regulations, there is a strong case for supposing that the curriculum they prescribed had been derived from one or both of these two earlier works, given their similarity. All in all, therefore, if any prior works enjoy just claim to be considered to be the true source of the National Curriculum, it is not the 1904 Regulations, but one or both of these two earlier works.

Why should it be thought to matter whether it was the 1904 Regulations or these earlier works from which the National Curriculum should be thought to have been derived? It matters because the two prior works base their respective curriculum proposals on entirely different historical precedents than the curricula of Edwardian grammar schools and eighteenth century Dissenting Academies. Moreover, one of these works offers on behalf of its proposed curriculum an entirely different rationale from the one which John White claims to have been the original and only rationale that the National Curriculum has ever had. If we are to decide whether it possesses a legitimate rationale in the form in which it was introduced, it matters whether it should be considered to have derived from the sources from which White and other critics of it claim it to have been derived or from these different sources which confer upon it an altogether different rationale from that which these critics claim it to have had.

To be able to make a genuinely informed decision as to how appropriate today the National Curriculum might be in the form it was originally introduced, two questions need answering. First, which works published before the 1904 Regulations propose curricula that resemble the one that they prescribed as much as it does the National Curriculum? Second, what rationale might either of these prior works have offered for its proposed curriculum? Only after having answered these two questions can the true source and rationale of the National Curriculum be thought to have been correctly identified. Without identifying these things, we shall not be in a position to know what might be the true justification for the academic subject-based form in which the National Curriculum was originally introduced or whether such a justification remains an adequate one. The remainder of this study is devoted to supplying answers to this crucial pair of questions that critics of the National Curriculum so assiduously avoid considering.

6

The True Source of the National Curriculum

Two works besides the 1904 Regulations enjoy the best claim to be considered the true source of the National Curriculum. They are *A French Eton or Middle-Class Education and the State* (1864) and *Higher Schools and Universities in Germany* (1868). Both works have a common author—namely, Matthew Arnold. Arguably England's foremost mid-Victorian social and literary critic, Arnold was also a major poet in his own right, occupying the Oxford chair of poetry for a decade from 1857. Less generally well known is the fact that, for 35 years, he was also a government inspector of elementary schools, eventually becoming chief inspector in 1884, a position he held until his retirement in 1886. Matthew Arnold was also the son of Thomas, fabled headmaster of Rugby where Matthew received his schooling during his father's headship, when a set of far-ranging reforms were instituted that rapidly became adopted by other English public schools and which did so much to modernise and humanise them.

In the person of Matthew Arnold, therefore, we have not some cantankerous, bile-filled university don, bent upon claiming for his own discipline some uniquely privileged power to preserve western culture and civilisation. Rather, we have a mild-mannered, gentle social critic with a life-long professional interest and involvement in education at every level. Although of impeccably middle-class background, Arnold always retained a deep and abiding interest in, and concern on behalf of, every social class in England, especially its working-class. Clearly, should he ever have expressed a view as to what an English national school curriculum should contain and why, it would be worthy of the most serious attention. Given that he did, its almost studied neglect by educationists today who claim that the National Curriculum is unduly academic and subject-based is nothing less than an intellectual scandal.

Arnold expounded his view of what an English national secondary school curriculum should contain and why in his two books about French and German education. He undertook the preliminary field research for each in his official capacity as a schools inspector. In the case of each such book, he visited the relevant country on behalf of one or another Commission investigating some aspect of English education. In both cases, Arnold was asked to investigate and report back upon the educational arrangements in the countries that he visited. It had been to investigate its elementary school system that Arnold had been sent to France. While there, he used the occasion to visit two French secondary schools in a purely personal capacity, as well as the elementary schools on which he had been officially asked to report. One was a lyceum in Toulouse. The other was a much older independent boarding school, founded by Benedictine monks in 1682 and situated in Soreze, a medieval town at the foot of the Black Mountain in the Pyrenees. Both of these schools taught an identical curriculum. Whereas the Ecole de Soreze had merely needed central government approval for whichever curriculum it decided to teach, the Toulouse lyceum was obliged to teach that curriculum which had been prescribed by central government for all French lyceums. It had been this heavily state-subsidised school which Arnold had been likening to Eton in the title of his work about French secondary and higher education. The main contrast that he drew between them was the much easier affordability of the French school for middle-class parents because of the large state subsidy it received.

Much of *A French Eton* was given over to detailing the curriculum, financing and organisation of the two French secondary schools that Arnold had visited in 1859. He published the work in 1864 in a purely private capacity. His purpose had been to reveal to the English public how far behind its neighbour their country had fallen in terms of providing high-quality, affordable secondary education for children of middle-class background. In doing so, it seems his intention had been to embarrass the Westminster Parliament into setting up a commission to investigate educational arrangements for such children in England similar to the other two Commissions that had previously been created to investigate such arrangements for children of the other two social classes. Parliament had set up the Newcastle Commission in 1859 to investigate 'the education of the poorer classes'. In 1861 it had set up the Clarendon Commission under the chairmanship of Lord Clarendon to investigate arrangements at the country's nine leading public schools. The Clarendon Commission published its report in the same year as Arnold published *A French Eton*. The provocative title he gave his book was intended to rub home just how much better was the quality of French schooling for children of middle-class background because of the large subsidy it received from the state and the much larger amount of state regulation to which its schools were subject.

Had Arnold's intention in publishing *A French Eton* been to embarrass the British authorities into setting up a commission to investigate educational arrangements in England for middle-class children, he would not have been disappointed. At the end of 1864, Parliament established a Schools Inquiry Commission under the chairmanship of Lord Taunton to investigate and recommend improvements in the education provided by the country's several hundred endowed schools. Colloquially named after its chairman, the Taunton Commission took three years to complete its deliberations. These resulted in the publication in 1868 of a monumental fourteen-volume report. Shortly after the Taunton Commission began its work, Arnold was seconded to it as an assistant commissioner. He was asked to visit several European countries to report back on their national secondary education arrangements, with recommendations as to how English secondary education might be improved on the basis of his findings.

Arnold duly visited several European countries in 1865. His accounts of their secondary school systems were published together as supplementary papers of the 1868 Taunton Report under the title of 'Schools and Universities on the Continent'. In that same year, Arnold also published separately that part of those papers dealing with secondary and higher education in Prussia. Of Arnold's two works in which he recommended curricula similar to that prescribed by the 1904 Regulations, it was this book about Prussian education in which Arnold provided a rationale for the curriculum.

This pair of works by Arnold was to exert extraordinary influence in England. To appreciate why, if any prior works deserve to be considered to be the source of the National Curriculum, it is these two that have the best claim, it is worth comparing the curricula they all variously propose or prescribe. The relevant details are set out in Table 6.1 (p. 47) which also provides details of the curricula proposed by the Hadow and Norwood Reports, as well as that proposed by Cyril Norwood in his 1909 book on secondary education. Table 6.1 also provides details of which subjects were prescribed by the National Curriculum in the form in which it was introduced in 1988.

In the case of the curriculum proposed by Arnold in his book on German secondary education, Table 6.1 has added drawing and singing to the list of subjects whose study was recommended. Although Arnold mentions neither in his account of the Prussian secondary school curriculum, they have been added in parenthesis because, when Arnold visited Prussia and found its prescribed secondary school curriculum so much to his liking, both subjects were parts of it. This fact was pointed out by the 1938 Spens Report.[1] Their omission by Arnold seems most likely to have been pure oversight.

Of the nationally prescribed curriculum Arnold had found being taught by French secondary schools, he commented: 'For the serious thinker, for the real student of the question of secondary instruction, the problem respecting secondary instruction which we in England have to solve is this: Why cannot we have throughout England—as the French have throughout France—schools where the children of our middle- and professional classes may obtain... an education of as good quality... as the education French children of the corresponding classes can obtain from institutions like that of Toulouse or Soreze?'[2]

Likewise, after outlining the similar nationally prescribed curriculum for Prussian gymnasia, Arnold observed: 'We have not... so good an education as in the higher schools of Prussia... The result is, that we have to meet the calls of a modern epoch... with a working class not educated at all, a middle class educated on the second plane, and the idea of science absent from the whole course and design of our education.'[3]

What did Arnold find so appealing about the similar curricula he found being taught at French and Prussian secondary schools? As we shall now see, what so appealed to him had nothing to do with religion in general, let alone Puritanism. Moreover, the features of them that appealed so to Arnold are ones the National Curriculum shares with them and make it so objectionable in the eyes of its critics. Such purely secular considerations as Arnold adduced on behalf of the curricula he proposed amount, therefore, to a rationale for the National Curriculum too. On the strength of the origins that have been attributed to it by some of its critics, it is claimed to lack any form of rationale but an archaically religious one. However, the origins these critics ascribe to it are at best incomplete and at worst fictitious. Once its true origins have been correctly identified, the National Curriculum can be seen to have a rationale that is not a religious one. What its true origins are is explained in the next section. The rationale that Matthew Arnold offered for a curriculum of just this sort is then explained in the section after that.

Table 6.1: Subjects Prescribed by Various National Curricula from Matthew Arnold's Day to the 1988 National Curriculum

1864	1868	1904	1909	1927	1943	1988
France	*Prussia*	*Regulations*	*Norwood & Hope*	*Hadow Report*	*Norwood Report*	*National Curriculum*
French	German	English	English	English	English	English
Geography	Geography	Geography	Geography	Geography	Geography	Geography
History	History	History	History	History	History	History
Foreign Languages	Foreign Languages	Foreign Languages	Foreign Languages	Foreign Languages	Foreign Languages	Foreign Languages
Mathematics	Mathematics	Mathematics	Mathematics	Mathematics	Mathematics	Mathematics
Science	Science	Science	Science	Science	Science	Science
Physical Exercise		Physical Exercise	Organised Sport	Physical Exercise	Physical Exercise	Physical Exercise
	(Drawing)	Drawing	Drawing/Art	Drawing & Applied Art	Art	Art
	(Singing)		Singing	Music	Music	Music
		Manual Training/ Housewifery (for girls)	Manual Training	Handwork	Handicraft	Technology

Source: France: Arnold, M., *A French Eton or Middle Class Education* (first published 1868) in *The Works of Matthew Arnold*, vol. XII, London: Macmillan, 1904, p. 11; Prussia: Arnold, M., *Higher Schools and Universities in Germany* (first published 1868) in *The Works of Matthew Arnold*, vol. XII, London: Macmillan, 1904, p. 399, and Young, R.F., 'Note by the secretary in the development of the conception of general liberal education', Appendix ll of *Secondary Education* (The Spens Report), London: HM Stationery Office, 1938, on-line version, p. 7; http://www.dg.dial.pipex.com/documents/docs2/spens13.shtml; England: 'Regulations for Secondary Schools 1904: Prefatory Memorandum' in Sylvester, D.W. and Maclure, S. (eds), *Educational Documents: England and Wales*, London: Taylor and Francis, first published 1965, fifth edn 1986, pp. 156–59; Norwood, C.A. and Hope, A.H., *The Higher Education of Boys in England*, London: John Murray, 1909, pp. 297–98 and p. 436; Consultative Committee of the Board of Education, *The Education of the Adolescent*, London: HMSO, 1927, pp. 188–89; Report of the Committee of the Secondary Schools Examinations Council appointed by the President of the Board of Education in 1941, *Curriculum and Examinations in Secondary Schools*, London: HMSO, 1943, ch. 8.; online version p. 17; www.dg.dial.pipex.com; Educational Reform Act 1988.

7

Liberal Education as the Purpose of the National Curriculum

Matthew Arnold (1822-88)

In 1868, Matthew Arnold proposed for all secondary schools in England a curriculum broadly the same as that which he had found being taught by their French and German counterparts. During the junior years, he proposed, pupils should be taught: 'The mother-tongue, the elements of Latin, and of the chief modern languages, the elements of history, of arithmetic and geometry, of geography, and of the knowledge of nature'.[1] In the upper years, he proposed, pupils should not only be permitted but encouraged to specialise according to their special interests and aptitudes. Even so, he insisted they should be required to undertake subsidiary study in whichever was not their principal field of studies. With the sole exception of Latin, the curriculum Arnold proposed is identical to that later prescribed by the 1904 Secondary School Regulations and by the Hadow and Norwood Reports. The subjects whose prescribed study he proposed also make up the bulk of the National Curriculum and comprise its more academic content. The only subjects that it added to his were music, art, physical education and technology.

Given how closely Arnold's proposed curriculum resembles the National Curriculum, whatever type of education Arnold considered his proposed curriculum to provide is one that the National Curriculum also can be considered to provide. On several occasions, Arnold referred to the type of education he believed his proposed curriculum provided by means of the expression 'a liberal education'. He was no more the originator of this term than he was of the type of education he used it to designate. Both have a far older provenance. It is an expression that is heard with ever diminishing frequency these days in public policy debates about education. Its diminishing use suggests ever fewer educationists and policy-makers any longer have much understanding of the kind of education it once was used to designate or how all-important at one time its provision was considered to be. It also suggests they are equally unaware that, in the form in which it was originally introduced, the National Curriculum too may also be considered to have been intended to provide this type of education.

Exactly what did Arnold mean by the term 'liberal education' and from where did both it and the type of education that he used it to designate originate, given he was the progenitor of neither? More importantly, why and with what justification did Arnold believe its provision to be the true main purpose of schooling?

In the introduction to *A French Eton*, Matthew Arnold described secondary education as 'the first great stage of a liberal education'; its 'second and finishing stage' being provided by university.[2] He further elucidated what he considered to be involved in its provision towards the end of his book on Prussian secondary education. There, he observed: 'The ideal of a general, liberal training is to carry us to a knowledge of ourselves and the world... The circle of knowledge comprehends both and we should all have some notion, at any rate of the whole circle of knowledge.'[3] From this statement, two inferences may be drawn about how Arnold conceived of this form of education. First, he considered a liberal education was a broad and balanced form of education, embracing both the natural sciences and the humanities. Second, he believed its provision required a suitably academic curriculum. It could not be either so vocational or so child-centred as to preclude systematic instruction in the various constituent subjects comprising the natural sciences and humanities. Several pages before he claimed the purpose of a liberal education to be to impart to its recipients such a broad circle of knowledge, Arnold had claimed its transmission to be the chief main purpose of education. He had stated:

> The aim and office of instruction, say many people, is to make a man a good citizen, or a good Christian or a gentleman; or it is to fit him to get on in the world, or it is to enable him to do his duty in the state of life to which he is called. It is none of these, and the modern spirit more and more discerns it to be none of these. These are at best secondary and indirect aims of instruction; its prime direct aim is to enable a man to *know himself and the world...* To know himself, a man must know the capabilities and performances of the human spirit; and the value of the humanities... is that it affords for this purpose an unsurpassed source of light and stimulus... But it is also a vital and formative knowledge to know the world, the laws which govern nature, and man as a part of nature.[4]

Given that Arnold maintained transmission of this broad circle of knowledge to be the purpose of liberal education, it follows that, for Arnold, the chief purpose of instruction is to provide a liberal education to its recipients. Until only very recently, this was also the view of practically all other leading educationists. In proportion as the original constituent subjects of the National Curriculum are being displaced by others deemed of greater social or vocational relevance, children in receipt of state schooling in England are being ever more progressively deprived of what until almost yesterday practically all of the country's leading educationists considered the main purpose of education. Today, the reasons they so regarded it are scarcely even considered by those calling for and making these changes to the National Curriculum. To bring home just how monumental and potentially damaging they might be, it is worth briefly considering the extent to which until only recently liberal education was taken for granted to be the central purpose of schooling.

Robert Morant (1863-1920)

Robert Morant, the first Permanent Secretary of the Board of Education, is widely considered to be the author of the 'Introduction' to the 1904 Elementary School Code and the 'Prefatory Memorandum' to the Secondary School Regulations of that same year. This is what will be assumed here.

The term 'liberal education' occurred in neither document. Despite not doing so, it is clear from them that, like Arnold, Morant regarded the provision of this form of education to be the chief purpose of all schooling, even though he recognised that it could be provided by the elementary schools of his day in no more than a rudimentary form. Thus, the Introduction to the Elementary School Code states:

> The purpose of the Public Elementary School is to form and strengthen the character and to develop the intelligence of the children entrusted to it... to train [them]... carefully in habits of observation and clear reasoning, so that they may gain an intelligent acquaintance with some of the facts and laws of nature; to arouse in them a living interest in the ideals and achievements of mankind, to bring them some familiarity with the literature and history of their own country... and to develop in them such a taste for good reading and thoughtful study as will enable them to increase that knowledge in after years by their own efforts.[5]

The type of education here stated to be the purpose of elementary schooling is clearly a general one. It goes well beyond being the most elementary or the most crudely vocational possible. Today, Robert Morant's name has become associated by critics of the National Curriculum with a narrow, elitist vision of the purposes of education. However, when the Elementary Schools Code was first published, that was not how he or it was regarded. A jubilant editorial in *The Times* stated:

> Now for the first time, the Board of Education makes... [public] in a document that reaches every elementary school teacher and many managers of elementary schools, a profession of educational faith... For the first time the child, rather than the official or the tax-payer, is recognised as the most important consideration; and for the first time official prominence is given to that aspect of educational aims which has, indeed, been recognised in our secondary education... the formation of character and preparation for life and the duties of citizenship.[6]

Other newspapers were no less fulsome at the time in singing the praises for what Robert Morant had written in the Introduction to the Code: 'The Westminster Gazette spoke of the new Code as an "educational revolution" and the Pall Mall Gazette called it an "amazing departure"... [T]he *Manchester Guardian* told its readers... "it is clear that he [Morant] is a man inspired with fine educational ideals and accurately informed"... Another educationist... writing for the *Speaker* recognised "the new tone... and welcome[d] with gratitude the substitution of definite and ennobling ideals for the mere tabulation of an assorted collection of subjects of instruction".'[7]

The Prefatory Memorandum to the 1904 Secondary School Regulations makes it even plainer that liberal education was considered to be the main purpose of the curriculum that they prescribed. It begins with the declaration:

> For the purposes of these Regulations, the term "Secondary School" will be held to include any Day or Boarding School which offers... up to and beyond the age of 16, a general education, mental and moral... of wider scope and more advanced degree than that in elementary schools. The Board desires to emphasise... the instruction must be general... Specialisation... should begin only after the general education has been carried out to a point at which ... a certain solid basis for life has been formed in acquaintance with the structure and laws of the physical world, in the accurate use of thought and language, and in a practical ability to begin dealing with affairs.[8]

Sir Cyril Norwood (1875-1956)

No less pivotal a figure in the twentieth-century development of education in England than Robert Morant was Cyril Norwood. According to a recent intellectual biographer of his, Norwood 'dominated a generation of educational reform and change in the early twentieth century' and was 'for more than four decades a leader in his field'.[9] Norwood was much more explicit than Morant in having acknowledged his agreement with Arnold on liberal education being the main purpose of schooling. He also provides a direct link between Arnold and the National Curriculum. For, in his 1909 book in which he proposed a curriculum virtually identical to the National Curriculum, Norwood quoted the very same passage from Arnold that was earlier quoted here about the true aim and office of instruction. Immediately after so doing, he remarked: 'Thus, forty years ago, did Matthew Arnold define the object which our higher education in England should set itself to attain.'[10]

Shortly afterwards, Norwood made a further observation in which even more conspicuously his complete agreement with Arnold was displayed on liberal education being the true purpose of schooling. Norwood wrote:

> For success in any walk of life, especially in a higher walk, there is need today for Englishmen with... a trained and quick intelligence... [T]his trained aptitude is the by-product of a liberal education, and it seems likely that Matthew Arnold... [was] right... such an education... meant a knowledge of oneself and the world... It is our first duty, therefore, to attempt... the elaboration of a course which shall give all boys of average ability some knowledge of both these realms [of] humanity and nature, *and the wish to know more*...[11]

It was with a view to outlining a form of schooling in which this type of education would be provided that, in his 1909 book, Norwood had proposed a curriculum for England's secondary schools. That proposed curriculum anticipated by more than a quarter of a century the one proposed in 1943 by the Schools Examinations Council, of which Norwood was the chairman, in a report that bears his name. Norwood's committee was approached for advice on curriculum and examination matters by R.A. Butler, President of the Board of Education in Winston Churchill's war-time administration, and a former pupil of Norwood's from his days as the headmaster of Marlborough.

In his 1909 book, Norwood explicitly stated that the central purpose of the curriculum it proposed was to provide a liberal education. He wrote: 'a Secondary School curriculum should be framed in view of the adaptability of the various subjects to educate the intellect and heart... Moreover, we hold it to be axiomatic that a liberal education, particularly up to the age of sixteen, means the training of the whole [child]... At school, the [child]... must be taught to know himself and the world, though in his last few years he will, according to his bent, devote his attention more exclusively to humane, or more scientific studies.'[12]

H.A.L. Fisher (1865-1940)

Less than a decade after the publication of Norwood's 1909 book, the scope of secondary education was to become widely extended in England through the enactment of the 1918 Education Act. This act raised the minimum school-leaving age from 12 years to 14. It also required local education authorities to ensure that there were enough secondary school places in the areas that they administered for all children deemed capable of benefiting from one.

The President of the Board of Education responsible for securing the safe passage of this piece of legislation through Parliament was the Oxford historian H.A.L. Fisher. He had been parachuted into Lloyd George's war-time administration in 1916 via a safe Liberal seat that became available through the death of its incumbent member and which Fisher had won at a subsequent by-election.

Fisher was not at all unfamiliar with or unsympathetic to liberal education as Arnold had conceived the notion. Nor was he at all averse to its extension to all schoolchildren in England, including those whom adverse economic circumstances compelled to complete their formal education in elementary schools. Fisher made known his unequivocal support for its extension to all schoolchildren in the parliamentary debates on the Education Bill. Speaking in the House of Commons in August 1917, Fisher declared:

> There is a growing sense... that the industrial workers of this country are entitled to be considered... as fit subjects for any form of education from which they are capable of benefiting... [A] new way of thinking about education has sprung up among the more reflecting members of our industrial army. They do not want education only in order that they may become better technical workmen and earn higher wages... They want it because they know that

through the treasures of the mind they can find... a source of pure enjoyment, and a refuge from the necessary hardships of a life spent in the midst of clanging machinery in our hideous cities of toil.[13]

Implementation of the provisions of the 1918 Education Act necessitated a massive increase in the size of local education authorities, as it did in the number of trained school-teachers. In a lecture delivered in Oxford in February 1919, Fisher explained what role universities could and should play in helping to satisfy these two needs. What he said on that occasion provides a further illustration of just how much he agreed with Arnold on liberal education being the true main purpose of education. What he said on that occasion has additional present-day relevance in light of the present government's ambition to increase the university participation rate to 50 per cent of all school-leavers and of the increasing emphasis it is placing upon vocationally-oriented studies at every level. Fisher declared:

> there is urgent need that the spirit of a liberal education should be infused into... [higher education]. Whether a large increase in the number of University graduates... will be a benefit to the State depends upon the way in which the Universities conceive and discharge their function... [I]f specialization is carried so far that neither Art nor Philosophy, the two all-pervading influences in any truly liberal education, enter into the ordinary work of the ordinary student, then very little will be gained by the enlargement or multiplication of our Universities... The business of a University is not to equip students for professional posts, but to train them in disinterested intellectual habits, to give them a vision of what real learning is, to refine taste, to form judgment, to enlarge curiosity, and to substitute for a low and material outlook on life a lofty view of its resources and demands.[14]

The Hadow Report

By the 1920s, it had become widely recognised that there was urgent need for a radical reorganisation of state-funded schooling to accommodate the vastly increased numbers of children now remaining at school beyond the previous minimum school-leaving age of 12. In 1924, the Board of Education appointed a consultative committee under the chairmanship of the musicologist Sir William Henry Hadow (1859-1937) 'to consider and report upon the organisation, objective and curriculum of courses of study suitable for children who will remain in full-time attendance at school, other than at Secondary Schools, up to the age of 15'.[15]

The so-called 'Hadow' Committee published its report in 1927 under the title *The Education of the Adolescent*. Among its principal recommendations were, first, that all children in England should remain in full-time education until the age of 15; second, that, until the age of 11, they should receive their education in separate schools to be known as 'primary' rather than 'elementary' ones; third, that, depending upon the results of tests at 11 to determine their aptitude, primary school-leavers should proceed to one of three different kinds of school which were all to be known as 'secondary' schools: 'grammar schools' for those displaying greatest academic aptitude and which, until then had been the only schools to be referred to as 'secondary'; 'junior technical schools' for the more technically-minded; and 'secondary moderns' for all other children.

The Hadow Report made one further recommendation of particular relevance to our present concerns. It recommended that, in their junior years of all secondary schools, they should teach a broadly similar curriculum. Grammar schools could teach a somewhat more academic variant of it, and secondary moderns and technical schools a more practical one. However, it was essentially a common curriculum that it proposed they should all teach. The common curriculum it proposed bears a remarkably strong similarity to the one Matthew Arnold proposed in the late 1860s, as it does to the National Curriculum in the form in which it was introduced in 1988.

When proposed by the Hadow Committee, they made it plain that they envisaged and had recommended this common curriculum to provide a liberal education to all schoolchildren in England. In their introduction to it, the Committee stated: 'The scheme which we advocate... is that between the age of 11 and (if possible) that of 15, all the children of the country who do not go forward to "secondary education" in the present and narrow sense of the word, should go forward to what is, in our view, a form of secondary education, in the truer and broader sense of the word, and... should spend the last three or four [years of their school life]... in the free and broad air of a general and humane education...' [16]

Like H.A.L. Fisher several years earlier, the Hadow Committee made it plain that it considered the main purpose of secondary education to be other than vocational. It was rather, so they stated, to serve as a prophylactic against what the Committee claimed to be the mentally cramping effects of the routine types of work typical of industrial societies. The Committee noted: 'Great Britain, like other countries... is passing through an era of industrialism... [that] demands too often... a narrow specialisation of faculty; ... produces, only too readily, a patterned uniformity of work and behaviour; and... unless it is corrected infect[s] the minds of men with the genius of its own life. Education can correct industrialism, by giving to the mind the breadth and the fresh vitality of new interests, as it can also make industry more effective.'[17]

It was to foster the mental breadth and vitality of the nation that the Hadow Committee recommended that all secondary schoolchildren in England should receive: 'a humane or liberal education... by means of a curriculum... [which] should have much in common with that provided in the schools at present commonly known as "secondary"... and only in the last two years should a "practical" bias be given.'[18] Its details were given in a concluding section of the report in which it was stated that:

> The school may be regarded as an ordered society in which... pupils are disciplined in certain... intellectual activities necessary for an understanding of the body of human civilisation and for an active participation in its processes. These may be regarded as falling into the following divisions: (1) Language, including literature and the arts of writing and reading. Under this heading may be included both the study of English in its various aspects, and that of a foreign language. (2) Geography and history... (3) Mathematics... (4) Elementary science... (5) Handiwork, including drawing and applied art... (6) Music.[19]

This proposed curriculum is practically identical with the National Curriculum. Its expressly stated purpose was to provide all English schoolchildren with a liberal education.

Sir Cyril Norwood (again)

In the year following the publication of the Hadow Report, Cyril Norwood published a second book about education in which he voiced his agreement that liberal education should be considered the central purpose of schooling in England. Entitled *The English Tradition of Education*, Norwood observed that a common curriculum similar to that proposed by the Hadow Report was in process of being introduced into schools in England. He wrote:

> In all secondary schools, whether free and independent, or aided by the State, or provided by the local authority, a curriculum which is roughly the same is being attempted... [It] is held to be the business of the schools to give a general education and that its subject-matter is tripartite: it must involve study of the mother-tongue, of a foreign language or languages, and of mathematics and science... On the basis of this general education boys are invited later to specialize along the lines for which they are best fitted.[20]

After noting the apparently spontaneous emergence of such a curriculum in English secondary schools, Norwood immediately went on to ask: 'What is the culture that is aimed at in the best tradition of English education?'[21] In his subsequent answer to this question, he reiterated his opinion that liberal education should be considered to be the true purpose of schooling. He answered his question by observing that: 'it is not the business of the school, it has never been part of the English tradition, to make boys at school into electrical engineers, or chartered accountants, butchers, bakers, or candlestick-makers: it is its business to train the mind, give a liberal education, and fit the boy for life, whatever his course is going to be.'[22]

Norwood was only too acutely aware that, to date, liberal education had been something provided very imperfectly on a national scale in England. He indicated his awareness of this towards the end of his 1927 book in a passage of considerable contemporary relevance. He wrote:

> It is possible for observers to remark, with more truth in their criticism than one likes to confess, that the community after half a century of compulsory education remains uneducated, and that it is possible to read and write and do sums, and be spiritually none the better for it... Today you may produce a masterpiece of the greatest dramatist that England or the world has produced, but you will not fill your theatre with the products of our State-maintained education... The crowded Cup-Tie, the throngs gaping and betting on "the dogs", the packed cinema—in these a democracy which has shown itself in action truly heroic shows itself incapable of accomplishment in the things of the spirit, and proves that its education so-called must have been either wrong or imperfect, a thing of quantity only, and never of quality.[23]

Despite levelling this scathing criticism at the low level of mass culture in England, Norwood remained confident the universal provision of an appropriately liberal form of education could raise the cultural level of the country above its pervasive Philistinism. He remarked:

The education that has so far been given to the people is at most partial and second-best, and has little in common whether in range or in spirit with the universal education that may be. It was but the least possible with which the people would be contented, and it was calculated to equip not citizens, but servants... But education has to fit us for something... so incomparably precious that it will save a man from being a mere unit, a cipher: it will give him a life of his own, independent of the machine. And therefore at any cost our education must never sink to the level at which it will be merely vocational.[24]

George Sampson (1873-1950)

In commenting on the low level of mass culture in England in his 1927 book, Norwood indicated his agreement with certain unnamed observers who had claimed England still remained an uneducated society despite half a century of compulsory schooling. Among those whom Norwood would have had in mind, George Sampson would almost certainly have been one. Like Arnold, an elementary schools inspector, Sampson was also a keen lover of English literature, as evidenced by his having been the author of the *Cambridge Concise History of English Literature* published in 1941.

Sampson was also the author of a once classic, now largely forgotten book, *English for the English: A Chapter on National Education*. First published in 1921, six years before Norwood's own second book, Sampson's earlier book is an impassioned plea for English to be made the focus of elementary schooling in England. In it, he argued that, when properly taught as not only a written and spoken language but also a body of literature, the study of English could provide all English schoolchildren with just the kind of liberal and humane education that the likes of Matthew Arnold and Cyril Norwood had claimed should be the central purpose of their schooling.

Sampson began his book with the very observation with which Norwood was to register agreement in his own 1927 book. A few pages in, he remarked that: 'with all its good intentions and its great achievements, our system of elementary education is a failure... An educational system that is not a failure will produce an educated population. The present system obviously does not do that.'[25] Sampson attributed that failure to insufficient appreciation by the general public that provision of a liberal education was and should be the principal purpose of schooling. He declared:

Much, indeed, has been accomplished in the past half-century of national education; but one great need has been forgotten. We have tried to educate the children: we have scarcely even tried to educate the public. Before educational progress is possible, the public must be taught the meaning of education…The national mind must be got to see that…[e]ducation is initiation, not apprenticeship… Education is a preparation for life, not merely for a livelihood, for living not for *a* living. Its aim is to make men and women, not 'hands'.[26]

Sampson illustrated that central thesis by means of a striking example. It is one with considerable present-day relevance, despite nearly all the menial jobs it mentions having long since become automated. What gives his example such relevance is the recent decision by the present Government to extend the period of compulsory full-time schooling to the age of 18. Many young persons who are about to be obliged to remain in full-time education or training would not otherwise have chosen to. In the overwhelming majority of their cases, the education they shall shortly be given will ostensibly be designed to be some form of vocational preparation for jobs for which, in a very large number of cases, no special prior training is needed, or, in many cases, even possible. Sampson's example was intended to show why all such forms of vocational education are precisely the very opposite of what the schooling of such future workers should aim at providing. He wrote:

When I go home at the end of a day's work, I show my season ticket to a man at the door of a Tube lift. I reach the platform, and, when the train arrives, the gates are opened and closed by a second man, and the train goes off, started and stopped by a third man. At the end of the train journey I show my ticket to a fourth man, and I go into the street, get in a bus, where a fifth man collects my fare and gives me a ticket as the bus careers along, guided by a sixth man on the front seat. Probably before the end of the journey I shall have to produce my ticket for inspection by a seventh man. Consider the lift-men, gate-men, motor-men, conductors; consider the steady growth of occupation in the direction of tasks like theirs, in which there is the almost mechanical repetition of almost mechanical actions! Modern mass-production does not require educated workmen; it scarcely needs even intelligent workmen. How can it be pretended that education has any specific application to tasks for which there is no need for intelligence? The lift-man would work his switch no worse if he were quite illiterate and no better if he were a doctor of science. It is not as a lift-man that he is worth educating, but as a man. That is what the nation must be persuaded to see.[27]

According to Sampson, to be capable of being carried out perfectly adequately, most modern jobs demand little by way of prior training. What this fact means, he argued, is not that those who will be called upon to perform such jobs do not need educating. It means, rather, that the education of which they stand in need is not a vocational one. Instead, he contends, it should be given over to preparing such future workers to be able to make worthwhile use of that part of their lives when they will not be working.

Sampson added another remark that is of no less relevance to contemporary discussions about the curriculum, particularly that for 14 to 19 year-olds. He asked:

> Is anyone prepared to maintain that the purpose of education is to teach boys to hew out coal and girls to put lids on boxes? I am prepared to maintain, and, indeed, do maintain, without any reservations or perhapses, that it is the purpose of education, not to prepare children *for* their occupations, but to prepare children *against* their occupations...We must really get out of the habit of talking as if education were the preparation of children merely for that part of their life which does not belong to them, as if they, as reasonable, living beings, had no existence at all... What is vitally wrong in the curriculum... is not merely the vocational inclusions, but the vocational exclusions... the exclusion of everything that does not pertain to vocation.[28]

It was Sampson's proposal that schools should reconfigure their teaching priorities around the need to prepare their pupils for their future leisure, not for work. He writes: 'Our schools for the young have failed because they have [not] tried... to lay the foundations of a humane education; and so the melancholy fact remains that, after 50 years of compulsory schooling, the Englishmen is still uneducated... Let the schools, therefore... abandon their so-called "practical" aims and their concern with some vague and disagreeable "livelihood" awaiting the pupils, and leaving results to time and natural development, turn their chief attention to the ideal embodied in that which, because its aim is to make men and women and not machines, we call the Humanities.'[29]

In claiming that elementary schools had failed to provide a humane education to their pupils, Sampson was levelling a most damning indictment at them, and by extension at wider society. To appreciate how great an indictment it was, consider what Sampson believed elementary education had to be like in order to be humane. It had, he claimed, to be: 'a gradual, leisured and comprehending acquaintance with that crystallisation of personality, life and experience which we call great literature, and with the history, science and philosophy that, in natural consequence, form part of the completeness of [that] literature. Such a progressive, co-operative initiation into the uttered and embodied life of man we call a humane education.' [30]

The major part of Sampson's book took the form of an elaborate plea for English to be made the central focus of elementary schooling in order that such a humane form of education could be provided by it. He argues that the ability to speak, read and write the language correctly, plus the ability to listen attentively to it when spoken, should be the main accomplishments elementary schools should focus on developing in their pupils. He declared: 'English is by far the most important subject in the elementary schools.'[31]

Sampson grounded that claim upon two principal considerations. First, English is the medium of instruction in England. Therefore, without competence in it, other subjects could not be learnt. He observed:

> *English cannot wait.* If a boy is not taught arithmetic or geography or science, he will simply lack arithmetic or geography or science for a time; but if he is not taught good English he will be perfecting himself in bad English...[32]

> In plain words and in the ordinary sense, English is not a school 'subject' at all. It is a condition of school life... Ability of the pupil to make a concise and lucid statement is postulated in our teaching every subject... [W]ithout clearness of expression clearness of thought is impossible... That is, progress in science, or French, or German, is impeded by faulty English...[33]

Sampson's second principal reason for wanting English to be the principal focus of instruction in elementary schools was that, since most native-born English children were likely to remain monolingual, English literature would be their only means of access to high culture. He observed: 'for the immensely greater number of English-speaking people, it is the only language ever learnt, and thus the sole means of approach to literature.'[34] Consequently, he argues: 'For English people, the great and immediate means of a humane education is to be found in English...'[35]

What Sampson wrote here about the importance of the study of English literature for those who do not proceed to any form of higher education is of great present-day relevance, given the imminent raising of the school-leaving age and the emphasis being given to using this extra time for vocational preparation. Sampson remarked:

> the obscure language of this little island has become the language of the world with a literature second to no other. But no attempt has ever yet been made to give the whole English people a humane education in and by the English language... [M]illions of boys and girls from the elementary schools and the modern middle class schools, and thousands of eager and energetic young men from the colleges of science and technology... pass into life untouched by the thoughts that breathe and words that burn in exhalations from the native soil. We do not give our elementary school children even so little as the decencies of cultivated speech.'[36]

Some today might be inclined to dismiss as chauvinistic and Anglo-centric Sampson's suggestion that the best way elementary schools could go about providing a humane education is by their focusing upon teaching English language and literature. However, Sampson was only being realistic in supposing the vast majority of the native-born English schoolchildren of his day would grow up monolingual, as they still surely continue to do in ours. Moreover, his understanding of English literature was not confined to such works as had originally been composed in English. He wished to include all good literature readable in English, no matter in which language it had originally been composed.[37] Given that capacious understanding of the scope of English literature as a school subject, Sampson was able to make the novel suggestion that the curriculum for it should include several of Plato's more accessible dialogues. He wrote:

> ... the boy of fourteen should be introduced to a kind of reading that finds no place in the usual scheme. I want him to make a first acquaintance with philosophy; and to put the matter in a simple and concrete way, I will suggest that he should begin to read Plato... Glance through the *Crito* and ask... first what there is in that a boy cannot follow; next, whether anything in our present curriculum provides that kind of reading; and next whether the process of steady mental interrogation, that gradual reduction of abstractions, either to thin air or to something actual, is not precisely the kind of education our pupils need and ought to go through... The process of that examination is the kind of discipline to which the average English mind is never subjected.[38]

In having claimed Plato's dialogues to be supremely educative, Sampson was by no means alone. In recounting the education he had received from his father, John Stuart Mill wrote of his first encounter with them at the age of 12: 'There is no author to whom my father thought himself more indebted for his own mental culture than Plato, or whom he more frequently recommended to young students. I can bear similar testimony. The Socratic method, of which the Platonic dialogues are the chief example, is unsurpassed as a discipline for correcting the errors, and clearing up the confusions incident to the... [mind left to itself]... under the guidance of popular phraseology... [A]s an education for precise thinking, [Plato] is inestimable.'[39]

Almost a hundred years after Sampson proposed that Plato's dialogues be included within the elementary school curriculum, neither the *Crito* nor any other Platonic dialogue yet forms a part of the curriculum for English schoolchildren. This is despite citizenship education having been made a compulsory part of the National Curriculum and the school-leaving age being about to be raised to 18. Their continued absence from the curriculum of state schools is deeply lamentable, as much as it is an indictment of the crude vocationalism that has become the obsession of the present Government in its approach towards education.

In recent times, no one has been a more forceful or effective critic of that single-minded recent obsession with the supposed vocational benefits of education than Alison Wolf. She has demonstrated how ill-conceived the idea is that social mobility or economic growth can best be promoted by encouraging or requiring ever greater numbers to extend their full-time education. Towards the end of her book *Does Education Matter?*, Wolf makes an observation of especial relevance in connection with Sampson's plea that a humane education focused around the proper teaching of English be made the central purpose of schooling. She writes that: 'Our preoccupation with education as an engine of growth has... narrowed... our vision of education itself... The contribution of education to economic life... is only one aspect of education... and it does not deserve the overwhelming emphasis which it now enjoys... Our recent forebears, living in significantly poorer times, were occupied above all with the cultural, moral and intellectual purposes of education. We impoverish ourselves by our indifference to these.'[40]

Sadly, appeal to the intrinsic benefits of a liberal education can be expected to carry little weight with those currently responsible for national educational policy. Perhaps, however, appeal to its potential for promoting community cohesion might. On behalf of the sort of humane education he advocated, Sampson advanced a subsidiary argument that might persuade even such keen instrumentalists as the present Government of its merits. This is provided that they are as genuinely keen as they claim to be about using schools to promote community cohesion, rather than as battle-grounds on which to fight what is effectively class-war by proxy against the middle-classes.

Sampson made his plea for English to be the focus of elementary schooling at a time when the class divide in England was very stark indeed between those whose education was entirely confined to elementary schooling and those who attended secondary schools and university. Sampson was convinced that, were his proposed curricular reforms to be adopted by grammar schools and even public schools, then much could be done not only to improve the education they provided, but also to abate class antagonisms. He wrote:

> There is no class in the country that does not need a full education in English... Possibly a common basis of education might do much to mitigate class antagonism that is dangerously keen at the moment and shows no sign of losing its edge... In the education of the poor boy and the rich boy there is nothing whatever in common except the profound uselessness of that education... If we want... class antagonism to be mitigated, we must... find some form of education common to the schools of all classes. A common school is, at present, quite impracticable. We are not ready yet to assimilate such a revolutionary change. But though a common school is impracticable, a common basis of education is not. The one common basis of a common culture is the common tongue.[41]

Sir Michael Sadler (1861-1943)

Since Sampson's day, the notion that common schools are needed so as to overcome class antagonisms has come to play a very large role in the educational thought and policies of successive Labour governments. Given the prominence of the comprehensive ideal in Labour's educational policies, it is interesting to note that the 1943 Norwood Report was not the first such report to have recommended the tripartite system. Although it did strongly recommend that system immediately before its implementation in the 1944 Education Act, it was, as we have noted, recommended earlier by the Hadow Report of 1927.

Among the members of the Hadow Committee who put their signature to its recommendation of the tripartite system, one was the

Labour Party's chief educational ideologue Richard Tawney. It was his 1922 pamphlet *Secondary Education for All* that was to serve for a generation as the basis of official Labour policy on education. Perhaps, however, Tawney's support for the tripartite system had only been tactical and was not altogether sincere. For, by early 1931, he had already begun to call for a system of comprehensive schools. In a lecture in March 1931, Tawney commented on proposed government spending cuts on education by declaring:

> Educational reformers in England have been far too modest... The time has come to be more trenchant and thoroughgoing. The objective of educational policy must be the establishment of complete educational equality for the whole population. Some children should not be offered a mean, scamped and hurried education while others are pampered. The odious tradition of class discrimination should be stamped out as a relic of barbarism.[42]

This assertion of Tawney's seems far more in keeping with Labour Party sentiment than was his earlier support for the tripartite system. This has especially been so since 1965, when Antony Crosland, in his capacity as Secretary of State for Education in Harold Wilson's Labour administration, issued all local education authorities in England with his famous circular in which they were urged in the name of equality to replace the tripartite system by a system of comprehensive schools.

Tawney's assertion was to be quoted and criticised a year after he made it by another eminent English educationist, Sir Michael Sadler. A fellow alumnus of Rugby like Tawney, Sadler levelled that criticism of Tawney in a lecture he delivered under the title *Liberal Education for Everbody*. The title of Sadler's lecture was a clear allusion to Tawney's 1922 Labour Party pamphlet. In his lecture, Sadler stated that: 'The birthright of every boy and girl in England should, in my judgment, include liberal education.'[43] This statement is yet another illustration of how widely by then the notion had become accepted that liberal education should be considered among the central purposes of state schooling.

In his 1932 lecture, Sadler gently berated Tawney for the economic unrealism of his educational proposals. He did so by remarking that: 'Mr Tawney is one of the saints of revolution. He carries unselfish generosity in public expenditure to a point which, if the electorate followed him, might mean civil war. I am with him heart and soul in the belief that every boy and girl in England, whether born in need or in ease, should have the fullest possible opportunity which education, in the widest sense of the word, can give them, but... think that, things being as they then were, to add millions to our expenditure on education last summer and autumn would have meant financial suicide.'[44]

Besides rejecting Tawney's egalitarian educational proposals on grounds of their economic unrealism, Sadler also rejected them for a second much deeper reason. It is a reason which remains highly germane in relation to current debates about equality of educational opportunity, as it does to concerns raised about the National Curriculum by those who claim it is overly academic. Sadler remarked of Tawney: 'When he speaks about education, he seems to leave out... a man's education is not only that which is imparted to him, but that which he himself achieves... The community... can help effectively those only who also help themselves... Therefore, liberal education in the modern state should... be manifold, not standardised... Liberal education for everybody... means making full-time education... effectively accessible to everyone. But it does not logically entail a corresponding extension of the period of compulsory attendance... There is no liberal education without sustained effort, self-denial and the spur of danger.'[45]

Sadler's chastening reminder of the decisive contribution to educational outcomes made by individual differences between children was given several decades after the publication of Norwood's 1909 book on secondary education. It could not possibly have been, therefore, because he agreed with Sadler about this that Norwood had chosen to dedicate to him that book by writing in its frontispiece: 'To Professor Michael E. Sadler, who, by scientific study of education at home and abroad, has more than any one, furthered the case of English higher schools and most untiringly voiced their needs.'[46]

The Norwood Report

Cyril Norwood certainly did agree with Sadler that children varied so greatly in aptitude as to warrant a tripartite system in preference to a system of comprehensive schooling. Indeed, the 'Norwood' Report was to recommend the tripartite system, although, as previously noted, it was not the first such kind of report so to do. R.A. Butler seems already to have committed himself and his government to its introduction after the war, before he approached his former headmaster in 1941 for advice about curriculum and examinations matters in connection with the post-war reconstruction of education in England.

Butler's prior commitment to the tripartite system was disclosed in a note that he made at the time of what had been said at a meeting he had with Norwood in November 1941. Besides revealing that prior commitment, Butler's note is of interest for an additional reason. It indicates that his former headmaster was still firmly wedded to the view that secondary schools should aim at providing a liberal education, even within the tripartite system. Butler's note runs: 'Norwood proposed that while his report would not study the technical and modern schools in detail, it would, however, indicate that all education for pupils over the age of 11 should be regarded as secondary, with a uniform curriculum for all those between the ages of 11 and 13, "so that all children at a later stage could feel that they had passed through the same mill at one period of their lives".'[47]

The 'common mill' through which Norwood indicated he wished all schoolchildren in England to pass was the common curriculum that was proposed for the junior years of all secondary schools in 1943 by the report that bears his name. This proposed curriculum, as previously noted, is practically identical to the one that had been proposed by Norwood in his 1909 book on secondary education when he indicated he conceived its purpose to be to provide a liberal education to all.

The term 'liberal education' barely figures in the Norwood Report. However, from what it said about the common curriculum, it is clear that it was proposed to enable all secondary schoolchildren in England to receive the rudiments of a liberal education. Its opening chapter states: 'in spite of differences, all pupils have common needs and a common destiny... and secondary education... must regard as its chief aim the satisfaction of all the needs of the child... Hence it would be reasonable that in the various types of school offering secondary education there should always be resemblances resulting from common purposes, but that in the early stages the resemblances should be stronger.'[48]

As well as being needed to satisfy the common educational needs of secondary schoolchildren, the Norwood Report also said that its proposed common curriculum was needed to facilitate their transfer between different types of school at the end of the junior period, should any have revealed aptitudes suggesting their better placement elsewhere in the system. The provision for such pupil transfer is often overlooked by critics of the tripartite system who claim that it ineluctably trapped children on the basis of fallible tests undertaken at the age of 11.

The only specific curriculum proposals made by the Norwood Report were for grammar schools. However, since it also recommended a broadly similar curriculum be taught in all three types of secondary school during the junior years, the grammar school curriculum it proposed for that period was also in effect being proposed for the two other types of secondary school. It stated: 'In the lower school of the grammar school we should ask for a curriculum comprising physical education, religious instruction, English, history, geography, mathematics, natural science…, art, handicrafts, music and one or two foreign languages.'[49] This is effectively the 1988 National Curriculum.

Having claimed that such a curriculum was needed to satisfy the educational needs of all secondary schoolchildren, the Norwood Report went on to make a further claim about it that takes us to the heart of the current controversy about the suitability of the National Curriculum. It declared: 'These are traditional subjects under traditional names; but we cannot replace them by any other subjects more "real" or more necessary or more desirable or more useful.'[50] As we have seen, many critics of the National Curriculum claim it is excessively academic as a result of being inappropriately subject-based. With growing success, they are seeing it replaced by one that is claimed to be more 'relevant' and closer to the interests of schoolchildren, especially the less academically oriented ones. One way that it is claimed it can be made more relevant and appealing is by not dividing up knowledge into what these critics claim to be arbitrary and artificial subject divisions.

The Norwood Committee was not unaware of the merits of multidisciplinary project-based work tailored to local circumstance. Indeed, one of its recommendations was that: 'form masters should have ample discretion to combine subject-matter as they can and wish, to pay attention to special needs, to digress and to take advantage of special opportunities which may be presented at the moment… [T]here should be freedom to schools to devise curricula suited to their pupils and to local needs.'[51] However, despite favouring such a broad measure of local autonomy and latitude, the Norwood Committee would have been opposed to a curriculum of the sort advocated by the likes of John White replacing a subject-based curriculum more similar to that proposed by Matthew Arnold. It would have been opposed above all for two reasons.

First, the Norwood Committee would have considered a child-centred aims-led curriculum to be entirely unsuitable for the most academically able pupils. For these, it considered suitable only a much more academic approach to their studies. One reason the Norwood Committee favoured the tripartite system was that it considered it could best enable children to receive whichever curriculum was best suited to their aptitudes in schools that did not have to be too large. When schools are small, children of different ability must be taught together in mixed-ability classes. To avoid this, they must either be taught in different kinds of school according to their different aptitudes or else in very large schools that go in for streaming or setting. In mixed-ability classes, progress is impeded, especially that of the most able. When children of different abilities are taught separately in very large schools, schooling becomes impersonal and the ethos suffers in consequence. Either way, the comprehensive system has an adverse impact upon the educational attainment levels of pupils. This was something of which the Norwood Committee was aware. It noted that: 'the tradition of English education has always valued human contacts and is not favourable to large schools in which the head master cannot have sufficient knowledge of each boy; thus a maximum figure is imposed beyond which expansion is undesirable, and in this connection it must always be remembered that there are far more pupils for whom a [secondary] modern school is appropriate than there are pupils for whom a grammar school is appropriate.'[52]

Faced with this dilemma of their party's own making, the present Government has consistently opted for large comprehensives. 'Since 1997, the number of secondaries with more than 1,500 pupils has more than doubled to 315, while those schools with fewer than 1,000 has fallen by a fifth to 2,119.'[53] Given the positive correlation there is known to be between school size and pupil indiscipline, a predictable consequence of these policies has been a growth in pupil indiscipline, with an inevitably adverse impact upon attainment levels. 'Official figures show that... pupils permanently excluded from the biggest schools in 2005... compared [to 1997] ... [underwent an] increase of more than a quarter. At the same time, the number of exclusions at schools with fewer than 1,000 pupils almost halved... As many as one in ten students from establishments with rolls of 1,000 or more are temporarily excluded—compared with three in 100 in smaller schools.'[54]

The poorer ethos of large schools, and the growth in their number relative to smaller schools, has been one major reason why so many state-educated children today trail so visibly behind their privately educated counterparts who invariably attend much smaller schools which typically select their pupils according to ability. The Norwood Committee was not un-alert to the dangers associated with unmanageably large schools. To avoid them was one reason why it recommended the tripartite system in preference to a system of comprehensive schools. The worst possible of all educational worlds, of course, is to combine mixed-ability classes with very large schools, a mode of pedagogy especially favoured by those opposed to the traditional curriculum.

There was an additional reason why the Norwood Committee would have preferred a traditional subject-based curriculum to one that contained substantial quantities of project-work and 'relevant' subjects like citizenship education. This was its acute awareness of how limited was the time available in school for study. The more of the curriculum that is devoted to project-work and to more relevant 'subjects' like citizenship education, the less time is available for traditional subjects. The Norwood Committee judged the study of these traditional subjects so valuable and indispensable as meant no substantial reduction in the time available for it could ever be justified. The Committee advanced two objections against such departures from the traditional curriculum as those for which critics of the National Curriculum have called. It stated:

> In the first place... premature attempts to deal with aspects of life beyond [the child's] experience can only lead to unreality and so will defeat their own purpose. Secondly, the very subjects and topics proposed [for project work]... depend for their study and appreciation upon the ordinary subjects of the curriculum, which would be largely displaced if all the [alternative] matters... were to become the subject matter of direct instruction. At least some knowledge of past history and geography are [sic] necessary to an acquaintance

with international affairs; vocational training needs knowledge of mathematics or science. There is a real danger that in the end the superstructure will become too heavy for the shrunken foundations, or that in preoccupation with ulterior purposes to meet the specific ends the immediate requirements of the pupil for general purposes will not be satisfied.[55]

This pair of objections against radical departures from a traditional subject-based curriculum provides a decisive rebuttal of those educationists, like Martin Johnson, Ivor Goodson and John White, who claim that it favours middle-class children at the expense of those from working-class backgrounds. It may well be true that, in general, the more socially privileged the background from which children come the easier they find it to master a traditional curriculum. Hence, it may well be that children from more privileged backgrounds tend to fare better in assessment on such a curriculum than children from less privileged backgrounds. However, that fact in no way establishes that the traditional subject-based curriculum is biased against children from less privileged backgrounds. Nor does it show in any way that it is prejudicial to them or not the curriculum best suited to their needs and circumstances as well to those of other schoolchildren.

The Norwood Committee claimed a degree of curriculum differentiation was warranted by the different educational needs and aptitudes of different children. Despite this, all children were judged equally in need for a good part of their schooling of a common curriculum sufficiently similar to the one Matthew Arnold proposed as to warrant being considered to provide, like his, a liberal education. Given the equal similarity of the National Curriculum (in the form in which it was introduced in 1988), the same can be said of it. This is borne out by what Kenneth Baker said were the reasons for its having been introduced in that form.

Lord Baker (1934-)

Nowhere in the preamble to the 1988 Education Reform Act, nor in the accounts Kenneth Baker has since given of why it included the subjects it did, is liberal education ever expressly stated to have been the intended purpose of the National Curriculum. Yet there are intimations in both the Act and what Baker has said about it that come close to stating that this was its intended purpose. Thus, the 1988 Education Reform Act stipulates that 'the curriculum of each maintained school

71

[should be] balanced and broadly based and promote the spiritual, moral and cultural development of pupils... and prepare such pupils for the opportunities, responsibilities and experiences of adult life.' Clearly, much of the reason why the National Curriculum was given its original subject-based form had been for it to promote 'the spiritual, moral and cultural development' of schoolchildren. Such a form of development is precisely what a liberal education provides.

That the provision of a liberal education was the intention of the form which the National Curriculum was given is borne out by several comments Baker has made about it. For example, in a Department of Education press release issued at the time of its introduction, he was quoted as having said: 'in this country, as nowhere else, the tradition of humanities teaching has continuing vitality and relevance. I am quite clear that every civilised society, to remain civilised, needs to develop in its citizens the aptitudes and intuitions which flow from engagement with the Humanities. The Humanities are an interrelated effort to give intellectual expression to the significance of what it means to be human.'[56]

Likewise, in the account that he offered in his memoirs about his concerns about the curriculum for English, Baker made it clear, without using the expression, that a central preoccupation of his was to ensure that it would contribute towards the provision of a liberal education. He wrote: 'It was because I love the English language and literature so much, and had drawn so much pleasure from it in my own life, that I wanted everyone else to have the chance of enjoying it... The only direct recommendation that I asked the National Curriculum Council to incorporate [was that primary school] children should... be encouraged to memorise the spelling of words and to learn poetry by heart.'[57] Baker recounts how pleased he had been at the time to receive from the then Poet Laureate Ted Hughes a letter voicing similar sentiments to his own on the value of the rote learning of literature. Quoting from a talk he had given, Hughes had written to Baker that:

> In English students are at sea, awash in the rubbish and incoherence of the jabber in the sound-waves—unless they have some internal sort of anchor/template of standards... What kids [need] who have no other access to it but TV, their pals and their parents who had only TV and their pals... is a handful of... blocks of achieved and exemplary language. When they know by heart 15 pages of Robert Frost, a page of Swift's 'Modest Proposal' and

'Animula' etc., etc., they have the guardian angel installed behind the tongue. They have... a great sheet anchor in the maelstrom of linguistic turbulence...[58]

Matthew Arnold would have concurred strongly with Baker and Hughes about the educative value of poetry in general, and of young schoolchildren being made to commit it to memory in particular. The Revised Code for Elementary Schools of 1862 had incorporated within the syllabus for pupil-teachers a so-called 'recitation' exercise. This required pupils to memorise so many lines of poetry each year and to recite them before the schools inspector at the annual tests on the outcome of which depended a considerable portion of their teachers' pay. In 1871, when English literature became part of the curriculum for the upper three grades of elementary schools, the recitation exercise was made a part of it.

Pupils were graded on not just how well they memorised and recited the poems, but also on their 'knowledge of meaning and allusions'. It has been remarked of Arnold that: '"the recitation exercise"... was one of the few regulations... for which... [he] had a good word to say.'[59] In his annual report for 1872, Arnold responded favourably to its extension to the upper three grades of elementary schools, writing: '"Recitation' is the special subject which produces at present, so far as I can observe, most good.'[60] Again, in his annual report for 1880, he was to observe that: 'Good poetry... tend[s] to form the soul and character; it tends to beget a love of beauty and of truth in alliance together, it suggests, however, indirectly, high and noble principles of action, and it inspires emotion so helpful in making principles operative. Hence its extreme importance to all of us; but in our elementary schools its importance seems to me to be at present quite extraordinary.'[61]

Having edited 'an anthology of poetry which told the history of England from Boadicea to Elizabeth ll', Kenneth Baker clearly shared Arnold's belief in the educative value of poetry, as well as that of requiring its committal to memory. Given how instrumental he was in ensuring that, in the form in which it was introduced, the National Curriculum also bore a close similarity to the curriculum Arnold had proposed in 1868, it seems that the later one may also be unquestionably regarded as having been intended, like Arnold's, to ensure that all English schoolchildren would receive through their schooling a liberal education.

Assuming that provision of a liberal education was the intended purpose of its original form, two questions remain to be answered before we can decide whether the National Curriculum should have been initially given the subject-based academic form its critics find so objectionable. First, exactly what did Matthew Arnold and others mean by calling the kind of education such a type of curriculum provides a *liberal* one? Second, why and with how much justification, did Arnold and these others consider the provision of this type of education to be the true main purpose of schooling? These two questions will be considered in the next section.

8

The Meaning, Origin and Rationale of Liberal Education

When, in 1868, Matthew Arnold claimed that his proposed curriculum would provide (the first stage of) a liberal education, he could have been confident of his readers having known what he meant by that claim. Such confidence is no longer possible. What Arnold and other champions of liberal education meant by this term is no longer generally understood. Such incomprehension extends even to some leading contemporary philosophers of education widely regarded as authorities on the subject.

Richard Pring's uncomprehending understanding of liberal education

Consider, for example, how Richard Pring has explicated the notion. Pring is a former Professor of Educational Studies at the University of Oxford and director of its Department of Educational Studies. He was also the lead director of the Nuffield Review of 14-19 Education and Training whose final report was published in June 2009.[1] He is exactly the sort of person upon whose views the country has come to rely of late in determining educational policy. It is precisely for that reason that his account of liberal education will be subject to close scrutiny in what follows.

Pring explicated the notion of a liberal education in a lecture delivered at the University of St Andrews in 1992 under the title 'The Aim of Education: Liberal or Vocational?'[2] In this lecture, Pring claimed that such champions of liberal education as Henry Newman, Matthew Arnold and Michael Oakeshott distinguished it from other species of education, such as the purely technical and vocational, by believing it to possess the following five distinguishing characteristics. First, its chief aim is to develop the intellect, understood as the acquisition of knowledge of and an ability to appreciate what was worthy of it, namely, 'the best that had been thought and said' in Matthew Arnold's memorable phrase. Second, such development proceeds by way of systematically organised knowledge normally imparted 'through subjects, under the tutelage of a teacher'. Third, the knowledge imparted must be of more than purely instrumental value. Fourth, because its acquisition is inherently demanding, it cannot 'happen incidentally' by means of child-centred learning from experience and interest. It can only be acquired from suitably qualified 'teachers already acquainted with the best that has been thought... free from the distractions of the immediate and the relevant.' Fifth, responsibility for its content, assessment, emphasis and direction must reside in the hands of those who have acquired their authority to teach from fellow scholars mainly working in universities.[3]

Armed with this account of what its champions took liberal education to be, Pring has little difficulty in disposing of the notion as he claims they understood it. To it, he ascribes the following pair of flaws:

> First, there is a mistaken tendency to define education by contrasting it with what is seen to be opposite and incompatible. 'Liberal' is contrasted with vocational as if the vocational, *properly taught*, cannot itself be liberating... Indeed, behind the liberal/vocational divide is another false dichotomy, namely, that between theory and practice... Intelligent 'knowing how' is ignored... Real science is for the able, craft for the rest; the science within the craft goes unrecognised, and for that both the able and the less able suffer.[4]

> Secondly... the liberal ideal picked out intellectual excellence... But... education is concerned with the development of the distinctively human qualities... possible only if the thoughts, feelings, relationships, and aspirations [of young people] are... not contemptuously rejected as of no concern to the tradition of liberal education. And that requires bringing the educational ideal to the[ir] vocational interests... educating them through their perception of relevance.[5]

What, it might be asked, is wrong with any of that? The answer is: plenty. To see what is wrong with it, consider the first of the two objections Pring levels against liberal education as he claims it was understood by the likes of Newman and Arnold. Pring contends that, in contrasting it as they did with vocational education, its advocates failed to appreciate that 'the vocational, *properly taught*, can be liberating—a way into those forms of knowledge through which a person is freed from ignorance.'[6] This claim of Pring's betokens a complete misunderstanding of how figures such as Newman and Arnold understood the notion of liberal education. It implies they gave it that name because they believed it to possess the unique ability to liberate its recipients from ignorance. However, that was not at all the reason they called the species of education they favoured a 'liberal' one.

It could hardly be thought to have escaped the attention of the likes of Henry Newman and Matthew Arnold that even the most crudely vocational forms of education also liberate their recipients from ignorance of one sort or another. For example, those taught how to fry hamburgers or to wait at tables thereby become liberated from ignorance as to how these things are done. Such champions of liberal education as Newman were not unaware that other species of education also imparted knowledge, in some cases quite advanced bodies of theoretical knowledge. Contrary to what Pring suggests, therefore, it was not because they considered that only liberal education liberates its recipients from ignorance that they sharply distinguished it from other species of education and valued it more highly. Nor was this their reason for having called their favoured species of education *liberal*. They withheld the epithet from species of education that they were fully prepared to recognise imparted considerable quantities of theoretical and abstract knowledge, and were quite happy to apply it to many other forms of activity besides education that have nothing remotely to do with imparting or acquiring knowledge in any shape or form.

Liberal education was distinguished from other species of education, and given its name, because it was sought after and acquired for an entirely different purpose than were they. Whether it was the receipt of education or some other more trivial pursuit, to qualify for the epithet of 'liberal', an activity had to be undertaken for some purpose other than to obtain a livelihood. Given what was thought necessary to qualify some form of activity as 'liberal', it automatically followed that no species of vocational education could ever correctly be termed such. This was no matter how intellectually demanding or spiritually uplifting it might be. All this was stated with pellucid clarity by Henry Newman when he observed:

> Many games or games of skill... are... liberal; on the other hand, what is merely professional, though highly intellectual... is not... liberal, and mercantile operations are not liberal at all. Why this distinction? Because that alone is liberal... which stands on its own pretensions, which is independent of sequel, [and] expects no complement... The most ordinary pursuits have this specific character, if they are self-sufficient and complete; the highest lose it, when they

minister to something beyond them... [A] treatise on reducing fractures [has greater worth and importance than]... a game of cricket or a fox-chase; yet of the two the bodily exercise has that quality which we call 'liberal', and the intellectual has it not. And so of the learned professions altogether, considered merely as professions... If, for instance, Theology, instead of being cultivated as a contemplation, be limited to the purposes of the pulpit... it loses—not its usefulness... not its meritoriousness,—but it does lose the particular attribute which I am illustrating... for Theology thus exercised is not a simple knowledge, but rather is an art or a business of making use of Theology.[7]

It was, thus, for an entirely different reason than that suggested by Richard Pring that such advocates of liberal education as Henry Newman distinguished it from vocational education. But having so distinguished it, exactly why did they call this species of education *liberal*, if it was not because they thought it uniquely liberated its recipients from ignorance? The true reason is ultimately an historical one. It goes all the way back to the inception of this species of education in classical antiquity.

The Classical Roots of Liberal Education

It was in Athens of the fifth and fourth centuries BCE that liberal education was first distinguished from other varieties of education, given its name, or rather its Greek equivalent 'paideia', and was assigned a superior value to other forms of education, in the sense of being believed to be the form of education ideally most worth receiving.

In an article published in 1998, W.R. Connor, then president of the North Carolina-based National Humanities Centre, purported to have identified the two earliest occurrences of Greek equivalents for the term. The very earliest occurrence of the term was said to be in a work from the fifth century BCE by Stesimbrotus of Thasos.[8] Although now lost, it is known to have contained a Greek equivalent for 'liberal education' through an extant essay from the first century CE by the Greek historian and biographer Plutarch. The subject of Plutarch's essay was a successful general named Cimon of whom Stesimbrotus had been a contemporary and written in the now lost work to which Plutrach referred in his own essay about the general. Plutarch wrote:

Stesimbrotus of Thasos, who lived near about the same time with Cimon, reports of him that he had little acquaintance either with music, or any of the other liberal studies and accomplishments, then common among the Greeks; that he had nothing whatever of the quickness and the ready speech of his countrymen in Attica;... and in his character in general resembled rather a native of Peloponnesus than of Athens...[9]

The next early work in which the term 'liberal education' was said to occur is a speech in praise of Athens dating from the early fourth century (c.380 BCE). The speech in question was by the Athenian sophist Isocrates, a contemporary of Plato's and someone whom many regard to be the true father of liberal education.[10] At one point in the speech, Isocrates declares: 'Philosophy... which has educated us for public affairs and made us gentle towards each other... was given to the world by our city. And Athens it is that has honoured eloquence, for she... knew... that whether men have been liberally educated from their earliest years is... made manifest most of all by their speech, and that this has proved itself to be the surest sign of culture in every one of us.' [11] Both of these early texts intimate that one of the principal benefits that a liberal education was originally thought to confer upon its recipients was equipping them with a capacity for eloquent speech. That intimation provides a clue why it came to acquire its name.

During the fifth and fourth centuries BCE, the native-born free male inhabitants of Athens became eligible for citizenship of that city-state upon reaching adulthood. In this, they differed from other residents of Athens: aliens, visiting citizens of other Greek city-states, native-born women and slaves. None of these were eligible for Athenian citizenship. Although, upon reaching adulthood, native-born sons of Athenian citizens became eligible for Athenian citizenship, it was not something that age automatically conferred upon them. To acquire it, they need to apply for it and successfully to pass scrutiny of their status and good-standing in a formal process known as 'dokimasia'.[12] Upon its acquisition, a new citizen of Athens became entitled to play an active part in its political life. He could attend and take part in the Assembly where laws were made and legal cases heard before citizen-juries. And he could stand for election by lot to the Council of 500, the body that effectively served Athens as the executive branch of government.

The vast majority of Athenian citizens were small free-holders or tradesmen, merchants, or craftsmen. All of these citizens needed to work for a living. A comparatively small minority were wealthy, slave-owning landowners who did not need to work for a living. It was specifically for the sons of this latter group that, during the course of the fifth century BCE, a new non-vocational form of education came to be devised and spoken of as a liberal education. Its purpose was to enable them to make the best possible use of the not inconsiderable quantities of leisure that they would have upon reaching adulthood. The form of education devised for them for this purpose was designed to impart to them such skills and knowledge as they were judged in need of to be able to put their future leisure to good use. Aristotle gave classic expression to the Greek conception of liberal education in his *Politics*, when he observed:

> it [is] clear that, in order to spend leisure in civilised pursuits, we... require a certain amount of learning, and that these branches of education and these subjects studied must have their own intrinsic purpose, as distinct from those necessary occupational subjects which are studied for reasons beyond themselves... Clearly then there is a form of education which we must provide for our sons, not as being useful or essential but as elevated and worthy of free men. [13]

Among the providers and purchasers of this form of education, a consensus quickly emerged as to what the best use was to which an Athenian citizen could put leisure, and hence as to what skills and knowledge were needed by those who would have lots of it at their disposal. Not all shared in this consensus. A small, but historically very influential, minority subscribed to a different, more elevated conception of the best possible use to which leisure could be put. The majority view was that the best possible use to which an Athenian citizen could devote his leisure was active engagement in the political life of the city, through participation in the Assembly and the Council. To enjoy success in these two arenas, the ability to speak eloquently and to argue a case cogently, or at least convincingly, was considered to be absolutely indispensable. Hence, according to those who subscribed to this majority view, the education needed by the sons of wealthy Athenians was one designed to equip them with eloquent speech and persuasive argumentation. Their generic name was 'rhetoric'. It was to acquire this set of verbal skills that many underwent a liberal education.

A minority held a different view of the best possible use to which leisure could be put. They believed it could not be spent in any better way other than by engaging in philosophy, or else in the still more recondite activity of contemplation ('theoria') that some believed was made possible by philosophical wisdom ('sophia').[14] Philosophy could be undertaken either in solitude, or else communally in the type of drinking-supper party immortalised by Plato in the *Symposium*. Such communal philosophising was both more customary, as well as generally speaking more highly regarded than was the solitary variety.

In practice, however, this local disagreement did not much affect the course of instruction that came to be provided for young men under the name of 'liberal education'. This was because, on either view of what the best possible use of leisure was, much the same set of skills and knowledge were judged necessary to enable someone to use their leisure to good effect. To be able to engage in philosophy with any degree of facility demanded a similar repertoire of abilities and knowledge as were considered necessary for effective oratory. Hence, regardless of whether it was ultimately to enable their recipients to engage in oratory or in philosophy, similar courses of non-vocational instruction began to be given to the sons of wealthy Athenians and to be spoken of as a 'liberal education'.[15] All who undertook any such course would be made to follow a roughly similar programme of studies. They would be expected to become familiar with the entire corpus of Homeric myth and other epic Greek literature. Such familiarity was considered necessary to gain acquaintance with instances of good style as well as learn about heroism and virtue. All such literary knowledge and skill came to be subsumed under the term 'grammar'. In addition, recipients of this form of education also underwent instruction in the arts of eloquent and persuasive speech, 'rhetoric', and of cogent reasoning, 'logic'. On top of acquiring these linguistic skills, recipients of a liberal education would also be made to study mathematics and physical science. They would be expected to gain proficiency in arithmetic, geometry, astronomy and music, with the last art being understood to include theoretical harmonics, as well as dexterity in singing or playing some instrument, typically the lyre. Instruction in all these various arts and sciences was considered necessary to broaden the minds of its recipients, as well as to provide them with subject-matter on which to practice and refine their rhetorical and logical skill and from which to draw in future oratory or philosophy. Whether intended to enable them engage in successful oratory or philosophy, all who underwent this programme of study did so without vocational purpose. They did not undertake it in order to acquire any form of expertise from the subsequent exercise of which it was expected and hoped they would derive their future livelihoods. Rather, it was provided and undertaken to enable them to make good use of their leisure.

The reason why this programme of non-vocational education came to be spoken of as a 'liberal' one was because it had been devised for free men, not slaves or servants, and it was intended to enable them to make good use of their free-time, not prepare them for work. Likewise, the several constituent arts and sciences that it was designed to impart acquired the generic name of 'liberal arts'. In late Roman times, the three linguistic arts of grammar, rhetoric and logic, became collectively known as the *trivium*. The remaining four mathematical arts, of arithmetic, geometry, astronomy and music, became known as the *quadrivium*. Eloquence was thought to be conferred by the first three; and erudition by the latter four. Acquisition of all seven arts came to be considered to be the product and goal of a liberal education.

With the Christianisation of the late Roman Empire, education became subordinated to the purposes of the church. When that empire collapsed, its provision became confined to monasteries and cathedral schools. There the provision of formal education largely remained during the long ensuing period of anarchy and disorder in Western Europe from which it did not finally begin to emerge until the beginning of the twelfth century. As life from then onwards started to become more prosperous and orderly, scholars began to congregate around cathedral schools and other centres of clerical education, some resident and others itinerant. Such informal collections of scholars became the nuclei around which universities came into being. They did so when local rulers began to authorise more senior resident scholars in such centres to certify various levels of competency in the liberal arts. Typically, such certification demanded successful completion of certain largely oral forms of examination administered by these scholars. The bachelor of (liberal) arts came to be awarded for a demonstrated basic degree of proficiency in them which was made an entry requirement for the faculties of law, medicine and theology at these places of learning. The award of a master of (liberal) arts was reserved for a demonstrated higher level of proficiency in these arts. Its award was made an entry qualification for the teaching profession.

By this time, the church had long since replaced the political arenas of the ancient world as the place in which eloquence and erudition was called for and displayed. Likewise, the more secular and informal modes of philosophising and oratory characteristic of the pre-Christian period had been replaced by what became an ever more elaborate and stylised mode of theological disputation known as 'scholasticism'. By this time, Latin had become the universal language of scholarship in Western Europe, Greek having long fallen into desuetude. There it remained until that great efflorescence of interest in Greek, and later Roman, literature and culture that began in the early fourteenth century and which lasted until the sixteenth century, known to later centuries as the Renaissance. By this time, the teaching of Latin, largely for clerical or bureaucratic purposes, had long become the central purpose of the numerous endowed 'grammar' schools that had sprung up in Western Europe, including Britain, often around cathedrals and monasteries.

Despite the Renaissance and the ensuing scientific revolution of the seventeenth century to which it led, England's two ancient, and for a long time only, universities were to retain their essentially medieval liberal arts curricula well into the nineteenth century, often in only a highly debased form. Only then did Oxford and Cambridge gradually begin to adjust and adapt themselves and their curricula to modernity. These two universities still retain as the names of their degree awards the medieval titles of bachelor and master of (liberal) arts. But they and other universities have long since ceased to reserve them for demonstrated proficiency in the liberal arts only. They are now awarded for demonstrated competency in vocational subjects too, such as business studies and accountancy.

The central point about true liberal arts programmes is that they were considered worthy of being undertaken for similarly non-vocational purposes as those for which they had originally been devised in the ancient world. In sum, the reason such broad courses of instruction in the humanities and in the sciences became called 'liberal education' was entirely different from what Pring suggests was the reason. It was not because, as he suggests, they were considered to liberate those who underwent them from ignorance. It was rather because they had been devised for free men and were intended to impart to them various skills and accomplishments they were considered to need to be able to make fruitful use of their leisure. This was why no forms of education designed to impart occupational skills were considered liberal, even though they might impart considerable bodies of knowledge. If a programme of instruction were designed or undertaken to prepare its recipient to be able to procure their livelihood, then, by definition, it could not be liberal.

The so-called 'liberal professions' of law, medicine and the church were so called by means of their preserving the fiction that their practitioners had acquired and exercised their relevant forms of expertise for other than mercenary reasons. Since the time of the Roman Tribune Cincius (c. 200 BCE), legal advocates had been prohibited by Roman statute from demanding payment from those on whose behalf they spoke. 'In later periods, as Roman law diffused itself over the great part of Europe, these restrictions upon the pecuniary remuneration of advocates... entirely disappeared... In form, however, the fee was merely an honorary consideration... Manifest traces of this practice are still to be found in all countries into which the Civil or Roman law has been introduced; and are also clearly discernible in rules and forms respecting fees to counsel at the present day in England.'[16] A more visible trace of the prohibition on payment survives in the gowns that English barristers wear in court. After Edward I granted monopoly rights to lawyers to speak in royal courts in England, they preserved the fiction that their motive was other than mercenary by having pockets sown onto the backs of the gowns they wore in court into which their clients, should they wish, could deposit a gratuity. 'The theory is that since barristers were not openly paid for their work, clients placed ex gratia payment into counsel's pockets, literally behind their back, to preserve their dignity.'[17]

Henry Newman on Intellectual Excellence

In light of the real reason why liberal education acquired the name it did, further and deeper errors become discernible in the account Pring gives of how this form of education was conceived and understood by such nineteenth-century champions of it as Henry Newman and Matthew Arnold. Identifying these errors will enable us to see how equally misguided is the second of the two criticisms that he levels against liberal education as he claims it was conceived by them.

Pring claims that, in having conceived of intellectual excellence as being the object of liberal education, such champions of liberal education as Henry Newman unduly restricted and overly intellectualised the scope of schooling. As a result, he claims, they failed to recognise that young persons possess other qualities and aspects of personality besides the intellect that are also in need of nurturance: notably, the emotions, feelings and relationships. Pring claims that this holds especially true of the less academically inclined young persons whose thoughts, feelings, relationships and aspirations he claims have often been 'contempt-uously rejected' by the champions of liberal education. Thus, he writes: 'Philosophy of education needs a more generous notion of what it is to be human than what has too often prevailed or been captured in the liberal ideal. Without such a notion... focus on intellectual excellence has ignored wider personal qualities, informed by thought, feeling, and various forms of awareness, which need nurturing, even if this must be for many in the context of the practical and useful.'[18]

Since first having levelled this charge at such champions of liberal education as Henry Newman and Matthew Arnold, Pring has repeated it on several occasions, including an article defending the compre-hensive ideal that forms the keynote contribution to an anthology published in 2008. Here, Pring observed: '"Intellectual excellence" is, for some, what constitutes an educated person... The ideal has been to introduce the young learner to... subjects in an ever more disciplined and theoretical way. However, the tendency, at its worst, has... disconnected [the subjects taught] from the cultural experiences that young people bring with them to school and with which they need to be logically connected.'[19]

The criticism re-occurred in the final report of the Nuffield Review of 14-19-year-old education and training. An early chapter raises the question of what counts as an educated 19 year-old in this day and age. After warning against confining this notion to the attainment of intellectual excellence, Pring quotes a sentence from Henry Newman to show him guilty of that equation. The quoted sentence runs: 'Liberal education, viewed in itself, is simply the cultivation of the intellect, as such, and its object is nothing more or less than intellectual excellence.'[20] Immediately after quoting this sentence, Pring observes that: 'care is needed, for often excellence is achieved on a narrow front (the cult of the specialist) and sits alongside ignorance of other matters which those deemed less well educated would be familiar with. Intellectual excellence is but part of the whole person. There is more to development and fulfilment as a person.'[21]

The account Pring gives here, and in all his other writings, of what Henry Newman meant by 'intellectual excellence' badly misconstrues how the latter understood and explicated that notion. As a result, what is claimed by Pring to follow from such excellence being conceived of as the goal of education is deeply flawed. So too are all the criticisms that he levels against considering such a form of excellence as the goal of education when understood in the manner Newman conceived of it.

In the first place, Newman would have rejected no less vigorously than Pring any suggestion that 'excellence achieved only in a narrow field' could possibly constitute a worthwhile educational ideal. For Newman, intellectual excellence was not something attained in direct proportion as knowledge was acquired, whether it assumed the form of some narrow expertise or else a smattering gained across a wide field. Newman explicitly asserted the contrary, writing: 'the end of a Liberal Education is not mere knowledge'.[22] Elsewhere, he adds: 'men who embrace in their minds a vast multitude of ideas, but with little sensibility about their real relations... may be learned in the law... [and] versed in statistics... If they are nothing more than well-read men, or men of information, they have not what specially deserves the name of culture of mind, or fulfils the type of Liberal Education.'[23]

For Newman, intellectual excellence consists in something he called 'a philosophical frame of mind'. By this expression he explained meant: 'the clear, calm, accurate vision and comprehension of all things... each in its place, and with its own characteristics'.[24] Such a frame of mind was said to require neither great erudition nor any narrow form of expertise. All it was said to need was the ability and willingness of someone to form as clear and accurate a synoptic view of the world as they could by reflecting on whatever information with which their experience and learning had supplied them, no matter how wide or narrow these had been. Newman writes: 'That only is true enlargement of mind which is the power of viewing many things at once as one whole, of referring them severally to their true place in the universal system, of understanding their respective values, and determining their mutual dependencies. Thus is that form of... Knowledge of which..., set up in the individual intellect, ... constitutes its perfection... To have even a portion of this illuminative reason and true philosophy is the highest state to which nature can aspire, in the way of intellect.'[25]

How misleading and inaccurate is Pring's account of what Newman understood by 'intellectual excellence' is something that can be gauged from the fact that, for Newman, it was capable of being acquired by someone, in principle, after their receipt of only the most rudimentary elementary schooling and with access to no more than the most modest stock of educational resources. Newman made this clear in a section of his *Idea of a University* in which he identifies 'various mistakes which at the present day beset the subject of University Education'.[26] He remarks there: 'I am not [for]... banishing... the possessors of deep and multifarious learning from my ideal University... I do but say that they constitute no type of the results at which it aims... [T]he practical error of the last twenty years [has been] ... to force upon ... [the student] so much [undigested knowledge] that he [has] rejected all. It has been the error of distracting and enfeebling the mind by an unmeaning profusion of subjects; of implying that a smattering in a dozen branches of study is... enlargement.'[27] This is hardly the view of someone for whom intellectual perfection consists in the acquisition of subject-knowledge gained under the tutelage of teachers which is how Pring portrays Newman as having understood the notion. Indeed, at one point, Newman expresses his preference for young persons to receive no formal tuition rather than an excess of it. He writes:

> ... if I had to choose between a so-called University which... gave its degrees to any person who passed an examination in a wide range of subjects, and a University which had no professors or examinations at all, but merely brought a number of young men together for three or four years, and then sent them away... if I were asked which... was the better discipline of the intellect... the more successful in training, moulding [and] enlarging the mind... I would have no hesitation in giving preference to that University which did nothing over that which exacted of its members an acquaintance with every science under the sun.[28]

In light of this avowed preference, it is hard to see on what basis Pring can claim that, for Newman, 'intellectual excellence lies in the mastery of... distinctive forms of knowledge...[to which] the ideal has been to introduce the young learner... in an ever more disciplined and theoretical way.'[29] Underlying Newman's preference was his confidence in the ability of young persons to educate themselves after their receipt of only the most modest prior formal instruction. He voiced that confidence in a passage which has immensely important bearings on the wisdom of the present Government's plans to expand 14-19-year-old education and to increase the university participation rate to 50 per cent of young persons. Newman wrote:

> ... independent of direct instruction on the part of Superiors, there is a sort of self-education... which... tends towards cultivation of the intellect... [and] recognises that knowledge is something more than a sort of passive reception of scraps and details; it is a something... which will never issue from the most strenuous efforts of a set of teachers, with no mutual sympathies and no intercommunion... teaching ... a set of youths who do not know them and do not know each other, on a large number of subjects, different in kind, and connected by no wide philosophy...[30]

The description Newman gives here of the kind of formal education he considers worse than none has about it a remarkable air of familiarity. It reads like an uncannily accurate and prescient description of much that passes for education in England today, where too many of its schools, colleges and universities have become borne down by governmental imperatives bidding them to increase their participation rates and to improve standards as measured by increasingly mechanised forms of assessment. It was because of his disbelief in the capacity of such kinds of educational institution to provide any form of genuine education that, at one point, Newman enjoins those in quest of one to shun them altogether. In a passage in which he drew on a favourite poem of his by George Crabbe, Newman went so far as to create the impression of having been an early precursor of those who, like Ivan Illich, have called for the de-schooling of society in the name of education. Newman declared:

> ... self-education in any shape... is preferable to a system of teaching which... does so little for the mind. Shut your College gates against the votary of knowledge, throw him back upon the searchings and efforts of his own mind; he will gain by being spared an entrance into your Babel... How much better, I say, is it for the active and thoughtful intellect... to eschew College and University altogether, than to submit to a drudgery so ignoble! How much more genuine an education is that of the poor boy in the Poem who... but ranging day by day around his widowed mother's home... and with only such slender outfit 'as the village school and books a few supplied', contrived from the beach, and the quay, and the fisher's boat, and the inn's fireside, and the tradesman's shop, and the shepherd's walk, and the smuggler's hut, and the mossy moor, and the

screaming gulls, and the restless waves, to fashion for himself a philosophy and a poetry of his own![31]

This passage reveals how badly Pring misrepresents Newman in claiming that he equated intellectual excellence with systematically organised subject knowledge imparted under expert instruction. It also shows how equally wrong Pring was to have claimed that, in having made intellectual excellence the goal of education, Newman failed to recognise, or do justice to, the need to cultivate and nurture the feelings and emotions of young people as well as their intellects. In speaking of the young hero of Crabbe's poem as having fashioned a 'poetry' for himself as well as 'a philosophy', Newman is clearly intimating that, for him, genuine education is as much about the cultivation and refinement of the sensibility as it is about cultivating knowledge. Newman is using the term 'poetry' here figuratively to mean, not a body of verse, but rather 'something compared to poetry; [such as] … spirit, or feeling'.[32]

Newman gave further indication that he considered cultivation of a refined sensibility to be as much a part of the goal of liberal education as the cultivation of knowledge, when he stated that, besides science, literature is the 'the other main constituent portion of the subject matter of Liberal Education'.[33] Despite his profound religiosity which made him regard much secular literature as decadent and corrupt, Newman acknowledged the works of such authors as Homer, Cervantes and Shakespeare as supremely educative of the emotions and sensibilities of young persons. He firmly believed no one, ideally, should be allowed to complete their formal education without studying their works. By contrast, Pring would appear to believe that, upon reaching the age of 14, young persons should be allowed to complete the remainder of their full-time education without having to study any great literature should they evince no interest in so doing. The educative value that Newman attached to the reading of such literature suggests Pring's belief to be folly. Newman remarks that, if allowed to complete their formal education without its study:

> … a pupil… [will have been] thrown upon Babel… without the honest indulgence of wit and humour and imagination having ever been permitted to him, without any fastidiousness of taste wrought into him, without any rule given him for discriminating the precious from the vile, beauty from sin, the truth from the sophistry of nature, what is innocent from what is poison…You [will] have shut up from him those whose thoughts strike home to our hearts,

whose words are proverbs, whose names are indigenous to all the world, who are the standard of their mother tongue, and the pride and boast of their countrymen...[34]

In light of a passage such as this, it is clearly ludicrous for Pring to claim, as he does, that, because of his exclusive preoccupation with the intellect, Newman failed to appreciate the need to cultivate the feelings and emotions of young persons. In order for their interests and concerns not to be 'contemptuously rejected', Pring claims that any curriculum they are made to follow must be one that is child-centred and vocationally-oriented. Such an assertion seems wholly unwarranted. For the entire period during which they are compelled to remain by law in full-time education, young persons are being considered to be not good judges of where their best interests lie in relation to their education. If made to follow a curriculum in whose design they have played no part, their interests and concerns are no more being contemptuously rejected than they are by their being required to remain in full-time education.

Pring favours young persons being legally compelled to remain in full-time education or training until the age of 18, even though many would clearly sooner be working or else, perhaps, educating themselves in the manner of the hero of Crabbe's poem. Well before the end of the current, much shorter period of compulsory education, many of them have already begun to exhibit a very strong disinclination to remain in full-time education. According to the government's chief adviser on schools in London, Sir Mike Tomlinson, as many as 25,000 14-year-olds regularly annually drop out of school in England in September at the start of the school year. This amounts to one pupil in every 24.[35] Truancy rates are also on the rise, with many young persons persistently truanting.[36] Given the marked reluctance that so many of them display to attend school until 16, in his favouring their being compelled by law to remain in full-time education or training until 18, it seems it is Pring, rather than Newman, who is prepared contemptuously to dismiss their avowed interests and often vocational concerns. His contemptuous dismissal of the avowed interests and concerns of this group of young persons remains only too conspicuous, even though Pring might seek to disguise the bitter pill of compulsion he favours their being made to swallow by giving it the veneer of child-centredness.

Sometimes the lengths Pring seems willing to go to win over and maintain the interests of young persons in their formal schooling border on the grotesque. For example, of gang culture he remarks: 'it would be wrong for educators to treat such cultures with disrespect, for to do so would be to disrespect those young persons whose identities and self respect are acquired, at least partly, through these cultures'.[37]

What Pring claims here is arguably the reverse of the truth. Educators properly respect young persons, who derive their identities and self-respect in part from gang membership, only when they treat gang-culture with the contempt and opprobrium that it so richly deserves. Otherwise, educators are pandering to what, in truth, are highly anti-social and potentially deeply criminal proclivities that they should be doing their best to eradicate. Are their educators supposed not to dispossess young persons in their charge of knives and drugs that they might seek to bring into school or college with them for gang-related purposes? One sincerely hopes that Pring would concur they may. Gang culture no more deserves being treated with respect by educators than does Al Qaeda or membership of Combat 18.

Of course, while so many young persons today in England begin their secondary schooling and often end it functionally illiterate, it might be thought utopian to be suggesting that, even until the age of 14, let alone until 16, they should all be required to follow as broad and balanced a curriculum as the National Curriculum was when introduced. However, the appropriate solution to this problem lies in primary schools focusing upon the more effective teaching of literacy and numeracy, and in secondary schools providing better and more intensive remedial education than they currently do. Where it does not lie is in the period of compulsory education being extended ever longer, while being made ever more child-centred and vocationally-oriented in a desperate effort to win over the attention and good-will of the less academically oriented.

John Stuart Mill on the Moral and Aesthetic Benefits of Liberal Education

One huge problem in England today is that so many children of school-age have been so badly parented that they begin school, and often continue, in so highly disturbed and un-socialised a state as effectively to be unable to receive any form of education there, no matter how child-centred or vocational the curriculum might be. The cause of this problem was long ago recognised by John Stuart Mill in a lecture delivered at St Andrews University in 1867 to mark the occasion of his election by its students to the position of honorary rector.

The subject of Mill's far-ranging lecture was liberal education, in particular, what someone needs to have studied in order to be said to have completed one and what the social and personal value of one is. Like Newman, Mill regards the proper purpose of universities to be to provide such a form of education, and not any form of vocational or professional training. Again, like Newman, Mill regarded the 'crown and consummation of a liberal education' to be the formation of 'a comprehensive and connected view of the things... already learned separately'.[38] However, he considers the formation of such a synoptic overview to be 'the last stage of a general education'.[39] To arrive at one worth having at university, Mill writes: 'we must be assured that the knowledge itself has been acquired elsewhere'.[40] Ideally, Mill thinks that such necessary preliminary knowledge should be imparted at school or, failing that, during a foundation stage of university. Like Matthew Arnold, Mill believed the knowledge imparted during the first stage of a liberal education should be broad and embrace the arts and the sciences. He writes: 'Short as life is... we are not so badly off that our scholars need be ignorant of the laws and properties of the world they live in, or our scientific men destitute of poetic feeling and artistic cultivation.'[41]

Like Newman, and, as we shall shortly see, like Arnold too, Mill also believed the receipt of a liberal education to confer innumerable benefits not only upon its recipients, but also upon the wider society to which they belonged. He writes:

> Men may be competent lawyers without general education, but it depends on general education to make them... lawyers...who demand, and are capable of apprehending, principles, instead of merely cramming their memory with details. And so of all other useful pursuits, mechanical included. Education makes a man a more intelligent shoemaker, if that be his occupation, but not by teaching him how to make shoes; it does so by the mental exercise it gives, and the habits it impresses.[42]

From this assertion, Mill drew the inference that: 'it should be our aim in learning, not merely to know the one thing that is to be our principal occupation... as well as it can be, but also to know something of all the great subjects of human interest... in their broad outline.'[43] Mill then proceeded to enumerate and explain the personal and social value of the various branches of learning and culture with which he believed acquaintance was needed for a complete liberal education. Having done so, he then proceeded to identify what he claimed were the educational limits of formal institutions of learning. The limits Mill specified reveal how badly Pring mischaracterises Mill by including him among those whom he claims restricted the scope of education to the cultivation of the intellect. Mill writes:

> It is a very imperfect education which trains the intelligence only, but not the will. *No one can dispense with an education directed expressly to the moral as well as to the intellectual part of our being...* [But] we must keep in view the inevitable limitations of what schools and universities can do. It is beyond their power to educate morally... Moral... education consist[s] in training the feelings and the daily habits; and these are, in the main, beyond the sphere and inaccessible to the control of public education. It is the home, the family, which give us the moral... education we really receive; and this is completed... by society, and the opinions and feelings with which we are there surrounded. [emphasis added.][44]

Assuming what Mill claims here about the inability of schools to supply pupils with any truly effective form of moral education is correct, what he writes shows how equally misguided are Pring and others like him who hold what they claim is an excessively subject-based National Curriculum responsible for most of the pupil dis-affection and disruptiveness afflicting schools in England today. These critics consider that its subject-based form is principally responsible for the poor behaviour and lack of interest so many schoolchildren in England today display towards their studies. Their proposed cure for such disruptive behaviour is to make the National Curriculum ever more child-centred and 'relevant'. Pring asks: 'How can *all* young people—not just those privileged with superior intelligence... or a culturally favourable background—find value in a culture which has so often been accessible to only the few?'[45] He answers that the curriculum needs to be made more accessible and relevant to the interests and concerns of the less intellectually and culturally privileged. He writes:

> Too much emphasis upon... the various subjects... results in Harold Wilson's comprehensive ideal, namely, 'a grammar school education for all', which, inappropriate for many, resulted in so much alienation from formal education...

The [true] comprehensive ideal is to extend to all young people the opportunity to participate seriously in dialogue between the subjective concerns of each and the objective world of meanings...[as embodied in school subjects].[46]

Should Mill be correct about how relatively unable schools are to influence the conduct of children in comparison with their families, then the chaotic domestic circumstances in which so many grow up in England today will have incapacitated them for the kind of dialogue Pring proposes as the cure for pupil alienation, even if offered the opportunity for it. That Mill is correct on this matter is seemingly borne out by the huge amount of disruptive behaviour and unruliness that occurs in schools before pupils have had any significant degree of exposure to the National Curriculum. For example, during the school year of 2006-7, more than 3,000 four and five year olds were sent home from nursery school in England for disruptive behaviour.[47] In that same year, more than 1,500 nursery schools pupils in England received fixed term exclusions. In almost a thousand of such cases, their suspensions were for having attacked a teacher or fellow pupil. Nearly 46,000 pupils were suspended in that year from primary schools.[48] In February 2009, it was reported that 'more than 300... pupils as young as six have been thrown out of school for carrying or using knives or other bladed weapons over the past five years according to... figures obtained from 16 education departments across England... The true extent of the problem is likely to involve thousands of children ...[since] 134 departments [were] unwilling or unable to provide statistics on knife-related expulsions.'[49] In April 2009, it was reported that: 'Teachers believe pupils' behaviour has worsened in the past few years, with children being disrespectful, insulting and even physically aggressive in the classroom... The problems appear to be worse among younger children, with a third of primary school staff reporting incidents of violent behaviour such as punching and kicking compared to a fifth of secondary school teachers.'[50]

It is clearly ludicrous to attribute such early maladjustment to an inappropriately academic school curriculum rather than the highly adverse domestic circumstances of the children exhibiting it. Until advocates of the comprehensive ideal face up to this truth, pupils at state schools in England will have to endure ever more unruly classrooms and an ever more dumbed-down curriculum that will increasingly impoverish the education of the more educable ones. Pring and others need to admit that the solution to this problem lies in a family policy being made more supportive of nurturing families, rather than in an ever more 'child-centred', aims-led curriculum. As has been noted: 'Children raised in single-parent households are, on average, more likely to… have health problems and psychological disorders, to commit crimes and exhibit other conduct disorders… than children whose parents got and stayed married. This "marriage gap" in children's well-being remains true even after researchers control for important characteristics, including parents' race, income and socio-economic status.'[51] The failure of Pring and other like-minded educationists to make this admission is especially tragic in the case of the more educable schoolchildren in England. For they are fast becoming ever more systematically deprived of a decent education in favour of one promising to be of greater relevance, and hence of greater appeal, to those who are less educable.

In no other area of schooling is the tragedy greater than in that which Mill termed the third 'main ingredient of human culture', after the two main ingredients of 'intellectual education and moral education'.[52] This is the area that he termed 'the aesthetic branch of culture; the culture which comes through poetry and art and [which] may be described as the education of the feelings and the cultivation of the beautiful'. Again, what Mill says about this branch of education shows how inaccurate is Pring to claim that Mill focused unduly on the need to cultivate the intellects of young persons, neglecting the need to cultivate their feelings too. Nothing could be further from the truth. Mill writes:

> If we wish men to practise virtue, it is worth… training them to feel… the absence of noble aims and endeavours as… degrading: to have a feeling of… the poorness and insignificance of human life if it is to be all spent in making things comfortable for ourselves and our kin… Now, of this elevated tone of mind the great source of inspiration is poetry, and all literature so far as it is poetical and artistic… Nor is it only loftiness… that [is] bred by poetic cultivation. Its power is as great in calming the soul, as in elevating it… Who does not feel a better man after a course of Dante or of Wordsworth… or after brooding over Gray's 'Elegy', or Shelley's 'Hymn to Intellectual Beauty'? … To whatever avocations we may be called in life, let us never quash these susceptibilities within us, but carefully seek the opportunities of maintaining them in exercise. The more prosaic our ordinary duties, the more necessary it is to keep up the tone of our minds by frequent visits to that higher region of thought and feeling.[53]

Schools enjoy no better opportunity to cultivate the feelings of which Mill here speaks than is given them by their having to teach a curriculum that requires their pupils to study suitably elevating literature during their formative years. As a result of the inclusion within the National Curriculum of ever more pseudo-'subjects' such as citizenship education and sex education, the scope for its study has progressively diminished in recent years. Likewise, the subordination of education to external tests has also diminished the scope for its study. In April 2009, it was reported that: 'Pupils are [now] encouraged to study short extracts of novels to pass exams at the expense of a more comprehensive appreciation of literature... Ofqual, the standards watchdog, said pupils could complete a GCSE [in English] without studying a whole novel... Dr Mary Bousted, general secretary of the Association of Teachers and Lecturers, said... "English... is no more. It has been replaced by a newcomer—literacy... For those children who spend their lives at home in front of the television... this loss will be incalculable".'[54]

Traditional subjects like English are today being forced to make room for more vocational and supposedly more 'relevant' and appealing ones. As they are made to do so, state schools in England are steadily becoming ever less able to cultivate in their pupils any form of nobility of soul or capacity for aesthetic enjoyment, save that for the least edifying forms of art and literature. This is an especially lamentable loss, given how rapidly in the case of most people does the capacity to appreciate art and literature atrophy unless it is exercised. Mill noted this point when he observed that:

> Capacity for the nobler feelings is in most natures a very tender plant, easily killed... by mere want of sustenance; and in the majority of cases it speedily dies away if... their position in life... and the society into which it has thrown them are not favourable to keeping that higher capacity in exercise. Men lose their high aspirations... and they addict themselves to inferior pleasures... because they are the only ones... which they are any longer capable of enjoying.[55]

Supposing Mill is correct here about how personally and socially valuable are the kinds of elevated feeling great art and literature routinely evoke, atrophy of the capacity for them through its early un-use is especially tragic. According to Mill, no more vital ingredient of human happiness exists than that which is provided by the capacity for such feelings. 'Next to selfishness, the principal cause which makes life

96

unsatisfactory is want of mental cultivation. A cultivated mind... finds sources of inexhaustible interest in all that surrounds it; in the objects of nature, the achievements of art, [and] the imaginations of poetry... It is possible, indeed, to become indifferent to all this.... but only when one has had from the beginning no moral or human interest in these things.'[56] In his *Autobiography*, Mill spoke of poetry, especially Wordsworth's, as being 'the very culture of the feelings... a source of inward joy, of sympathetic and imaginative pleasure, which could be shared in by all human beings... [and] the perennial sources of happiness, when all the greater evils of life shall have been removed'.[57]

Mill firmly believed there was 'absolutely no reason in the nature of things why an amount of mental culture sufficient to give an intelligent interest in these objects of contemplation should not be the inheritance of every one born in a civilised country.'[58] He had not reckoned on some of the politicians and educationists we have today who together have been able to engineer public acceptance of changes to the National Curriculum that have made it increasingly difficult for state schools to be able to cultivate the moral imaginations of their pupils by engaging them in the study of great literature.

Some might be inclined to doubt whether the current period of compulsory school attendance is sufficiently long to equip those who might choose to leave school at the earliest opportunity with an adequately formative aesthetic education. In relation to that doubt, it is worth noting that even so elevated an apostle of liberal education as F.R. Leavis claimed that 'an intelligent study of *Huckleberry Finn* [along] ... with a study of Mark Twain and Mark Twain's America... offers as good an entry into the study of civilised man, and of the problems of civilised living, as a scheme of liberal education could ask for.'[59]

Even so seemingly an accessible form of liberal education as one organised around *Huckleberry Finn,* or some equivalent novel by an English author like Austen or Dickens, would appear to be still too elitist and exclusionary for the likes of many present-day educationists. So long as children are taught a curriculum in whose design they have played no part, their view seems to be that not enough voice will have been given to children in its design to justify it. Pring seemingly commits himself to this view in his 1992 lecture by remarking that: 'the tradition of liberal education which we have inherited writes off too many young people... Their voices are not allowed into the conversation, and the voices they listen to are not considered to be among "the best that has been thought and said"... Perhaps, the tradition itself needs to be re-examined.'[60] It has been a constant theme of his that those undergoing education should enjoy as much voice as their educators over what they should be made to study. In 2008, Pring warned that: 'picking out certain ways of knowing, understanding and feeling as somehow illuminating and life-enhancing... is constantly in danger of... creating an "educational elite", a people set apart, with a contempt for those not within the cultural circles... Certain... art, music and literature... are picked out as objectively superior—[as] the high culture.'[61] According to Pring, no such form of selection admits of adequate justification. He writes that:

> There is not, nor ever will there be, consensus over what literature is most worth reading or what period (and location) of history is most worth studying or which subjects most worth struggling with... In the absence of moral expertise, the exploration of what it is to be human is to be shared... between student and teacher... if each student... is to be taken seriously.[62]

By the time the final report of the Nuffield Review of 14-19-year-old education was published in June 2009, so strongly had the tide of opinion seemingly begun to turn in Pring's favour that he was able to report there was 'good news' that: 'There is increasing... recognition of the need to adapt the curriculum to... the individual learner, to take seriously his or her voice and experience... [T]he contrasting approach [is] where learning happens... with a curriculum divided exclusively into subjects, [and] with the teacher dominating the content and method of learning...' [63]

Matthew Arnold on Culture as the Goal and Rationale of Liberal Education

Pring's scepticism that no curriculum could ever command universal assent is one shared by many other critics of the National Curriculum who like him consider it was unduly academic in the subject-based form in which it was introduced. The prevalence of their scepticism constitutes, perhaps, today the single greatest obstacle to liberal education once again becoming widely accepted as the central purpose of schooling. So long as it is becoming ever more widely accepted that any academic subject-based curriculum represents nothing more than the arbitrary cultural preferences of whoever has devised it, so will the prospects steadily diminish that all schoolchildren in England shall ever be able to receive the kind of education Matthew Arnold and other champions of liberal education recommended. This is because their conception of a liberal education was predicated on the assumption that there would always be sufficient consensus on what was 'the best that had been thought and said' as to permit the identification of a canon that all undergoing education should study.

Pring, and others like him, might well be correct in supposing there will never be universal agreement on which literature is most worth reading. The crucial question, however, is whether it follows that schoolchildren should be given as much say as those responsible for their education as to what literature they should study. This is an entirely different matter. From a lack of consensus within medicine as to which possible treatment is the best in respect of every disease, few would wish to infer that medical opinion on such matters should carry no greater weight than lay opinion. It is unclear then why a corresponding lack of consensus among literary scholars and historians as to which works and periods are most worth studying should be thought to establish that their opinions should count for no more than those of young persons without any literary or historical expertise. If, for historical or political reasons, a country has decided to have a national curriculum, then what it should contain should be left to those with the appropriate expertise and authority to decide such matters. It should not be decided by those yet to complete their schooling.

The supposed experts might never be able to agree on what the ideal curriculum should be for those undergoing education. Such lack of agreement does not establish that those undergoing education should have as much say on what they should study as those responsible for their education. It only shows that hard choices will always have to be made by those with the appropriate expertise and authority to make them. Such requisite expertise and authority is precisely what schoolchildren lack. Everyone who has ever been called upon to help devise a curriculum will know that it can be, and typically is, the occasion for deep disagreement between those involved. Often the resulting curricula represent no more than uneasy compromises between the various contending parties, judged less than ideal by all of them. None of these facts in any way show that, because of such lack of agreement, students should be accorded equal say concerning what they should study as their teachers and others with appropriate expertise and authority to decide these matters.

Who qualifies in some academic field as an expert is a matter on which, at any given time, there can be considerable consensus among scholars within a country, despite their disagreement on many major issues within their field. Such consensus emerges through peer review and various forms of certification and academic award and honour, both formal and informal. There is nothing, in principle, to prevent scholars from being able to acknowledge expertise in their fields, even when they disagree with the opinions of those whose expertise they acknowledge. Despite frequent huge disagreements between scholars in every discipline, there is, typically, at the same time much agreement on a whole range of issues pertaining to them. Such agreement encompasses such matters as who, within their discipline, currently enjoys the most peer recognition; which works and authors have been of the greatest influence in its development; and which works need to be studied by those undergoing instruction in them and in what approximate order. Much agreement can coexist among scholars, therefore, alongside massive and deep scholarly disagreement. Within practically every major field of human thought and endeavour, at every level from the most elementary to the most advanced, it is typically possible for those with appropriate expertise to be able to select which works, topics and authors should receive the attention of those engaged in their study, and in what order.

At this point, we need to recall what Matthew Arnold stated to be the true main purpose of schooling. He claimed its main purpose should be to provide those in receipt of it with knowledge of human capability and achievement and of the workings of nature. Knowledge of the former was said to be obtained through study of the humanities; knowledge of the latter through study of the natural sciences. There is one fundamental difference between the humanities and the natural sciences which has a bearing on what the study of each of these sets of disciplines involves. The natural sciences are progressive in a way in which the humanities are not. In the case of the natural sciences, successive theories gain general acceptance because they are judged to possess greater verisimilitude than their predecessors.[64] In the case of the humanities, similar change takes place in terms of which authors, issues and approaches enjoy most currency at any given time among recognised scholars within the relevant fields. However, such change is not regulated by any principle that corresponds with that of verisimilitude. Consequently, in the case of the humanities, once any works or authors have once come to achieve seminal importance, they rarely cease to be of interest to scholars in the relevant disciplines. This contrasts with the natural sciences, where supplanted theories typically cease to be of anything but historical interest. For example, the theory of phlogiston and the geo-centric conception of the universe are today of no more than historical interest. By contrast, the works of Plato and Shakespeare remain today of as much interest to literary scholars and philosophers as any contemporary works in their subjects. These classic works are considered to be as much sources of insight and worthy of continued study as are any contemporary works. This means that, in the case of the humanities, unlike in the case of the natural sciences, there develop canons of work of perennial interest. Typically, study of any humanities discipline involves progressively wider acquaintance with an ever larger portion of its received canon, as well as ever deeper acquaintance with some particular portion of it.

For someone to become acquainted with 'the best that has been thought and said' in the humanities and the natural sciences is for them to acquire what Matthew Arnold famously termed 'culture'. The product and purpose of its acquisition was never thought to be mere inert knowledge of what some esteemed figures from the past and present have thought and written. For Arnold, the effect and purpose of the acquisition of culture was always practical rather than theoretical, affective rather than cognitive.

In the same year as his book about Prussian education was published, Arnold also published what, perhaps, is his best known work, *Culture and Anarchy*. In its preface, Arnold stated his purpose in writing it had been 'to recommend culture as the great help out of our present difficulties'.[65] The difficulties to which he there averred were the growing anarchy he believed must inexorably attend the rise of liberal democracy unless it could be contained by a higher purpose that he believed only culture was capable supplying. In so arguing, Arnold had been much influenced and shaken by the 'Hyde Park riots' of 1866, when 'a large crowd attending a meeting of the Reform League got out of hand and broke down the iron railings surrounding Hyde Park'.[66] Arnold regarded this act of public disorder to be a harbinger of worse to come, unless society could be united and made more law-abiding and civil by the moral and spiritual elevation he believed the acquisition of culture in his sense could supply. Thus, he observed:

> Freedom... [is] one of those things which we worshipped in itself, without enough regarding the ends for which freedom is to be desired... Evidently... we are in danger of drifting towards anarchy... [T]he Hyde Park rough... [was] just asserting his personal liberty a little... [but is in danger of falling] into the habit ... oftener and oftener... and so... increas[ing]... anarchy and social disinte-gration... Now, if culture... shows us that there is nothing so very blessed in merely doing as one likes... then we have got a... much wanted principle... of authority, to counteract the tendency to anarchy which seems to be threatening us... The very principle of the authority which we are seeking as defence against anarchy is right reason, ideas, light.[67]

Some today might be tempted to scoff at what they will consider to be Arnold's naivety in having supposed culture to be capable of preventing social unrest, as they also might be at his seeming undue fearfulness of ever-increasing public disorder unless it was prevented by the wider dissemination of culture. Arguably, however, Arnold was being neither naïve nor overly fearful.

Arnold was not being naïve because he never believed culture by itself could combat or prevent social disorder. He always acknowledged the perennial need for robust law-enforcement by the state. Thus, he observed: 'Because a State in which law is authoritative and sovereign... is requisite, if man is to bring to maturity anything precious and lasting in our eyes, the State... is sacred... [and] for resisting anarchy the lovers of culture may prize and employ fire and strength.'[68]

Similarly, in having believed that liberal democracy must issue in ever greater anarchy and disorder unless tempered by culture Arnold was not being overly fearful. As Christie Davies has well documented, during the course of the second half of the nineteenth century, the rates of crime and public disorder in England and Wales fell very rapidly and dramatically, especially among the young and to much lower levels than they are at present.[69] Thus, Davies notes:

> The overall incidence of serious offences recorded by police in the 1890s was only about 60 percent of what it had been in the 1850s... Trials for all indictable crime fell from an annual average of 288 trials per 100,000 of the population in the early 1860s to only 164 per 100,000 in the late 1890s... [F]urther...criminals were getting older. The prison population in particular was on average older at the end of the nineteenth century than it had been earlier... There were fewer

juvenile recruits to crime at time when crime was falling... Crime had fallen fastest among the young. It is a striking obverse to the rise of the youthful criminal in the latter part of the twentieth century. [70]

This period was one which also saw a massive expansion in elementary schooling. This expansion occurred at a time when it was taken for granted that a central purpose of such schooling would be the nurturance of faith and morals through study of the Bible. It was also a time when practically all children were born within wedlock and grew up in two-parent households in which religion was reinforced through regular prayer and church attendance and decorum and moral decency strongly reinforced.[71] It has, arguably, not been any coincidence that, since the time state-schools ceased attempting to nurture faith from the 1960s onwards, both marriage and organised religion have become increasingly unpopular.

Consider, for example, changes that have taken place in England in the illegitimacy ratio, that is, the proportion of out-of-wedlock births to total births there. It fell from a peak of seven per cent in 1847 to under four per cent by 1900. Apart from the exception of the two world wars, it remained at around the five per cent mark until 1960.[72] 'It then started a rapid rise: to over eight per cent in 1970, 12 per cent in 1980, and then... to more than 32 per cent by the end of 1992—a six-fold rise in three decades.'[73] The illegitimacy ratio has continued to increase in Britain. It increased from 38.7 per cent in 1996 to 49.4 per cent in 2006. It is now thought to exceed 50 per cent.[74]

A similar precipitous decline has occurred in terms of religious observance. Writing in 2001, Callum G. Brown, Reader in History at the University of Strathcylde, noted that: 'In unprecedented numbers, the British people since the 1960s have stopped going to church, have allowed their church membership to lapse, have stopped marrying in church and have neglected to baptise their children. Meanwhile, their children, the two generations who grew to maturity in the last 30 years of the twentieth century, stopped going to Sunday school, stopped entering confirmation or communicant classes, and rarely, if ever, stepped inside a church to worship in their entire lives. The cycle of inter-generational renewal of Christian affiliation... was permanently disrupted in the "swinging sixties".'[75]

As marriage and religious observance have fallen away, so has the country witnessed a massive increase in drunkenness, unruliness, foul language, rudeness, incivility and gratuitous violence, especially on the part of the young. Christie Davies writes: 'In 1957, just over half a million notifiable offences were recorded by the police, and in 1997 just under four and a half million. In 1957, just under 11,000 crimes of violence against the person were recorded and in 1997 a quarter of a million. Recorded crime in general in 1997 was seven times as high as it had been in 1957 and violent crime was 20 times as high.... Even if we allow for the rise in population there were nearly 30 times as many crimes recorded in 1997 as in 1900 and most of the increase occurred after 1955.'[76] Since Labour came to power in 1997, there has been a 70 per cent rise in violent crime.[77]

Arnold considered religion to be an integral element of culture and religious instruction to be 'more indispensable in the public[ly maintained] school than in any other'.[78] In his 1873 book *Literature and Dogma*, he observed that: 'of conduct, which is more than three-fourths of human life, the Bible, whatever people may thus think and say, is the great inspirer... The very power of religion... lies in its bringing *emotion* to bear on our rules of conduct... [so] that we [can] surmount the great practical difficulty of acting in obedience to them, and follow them heartily and easily.'[79] Arnold always remained much exercised by the prospect of the demoralisation of society that he was convinced must inexorably attend its complete secularisation. He argued that the state should harness the human susceptibility to religion so as to promote morality. He wrote: 'The power which has to govern men, must not omit to take account of one of the most powerful motors of men's nature, their religious feeling.'[80] In the case of state schools, Arnold believed the susceptibility of pupils to religious belief should be drawn upon for the purpose of their moralisation by means of appropriate Bible study. In his 1869 General Report on elementary schools, Arnold urged such schools should be made to:

> ... make the main outlines of Bible history, and the getting by heart a selection of the finest Psalms, the most interesting passages from the historical and prophetical books of the Old Testament, and the chief parables, discourses, and exhortations of the New, a part of the regular school work... [Such] use of the Bible... is the only chance for saving the one elevating and inspiring element in the scanty instruction of our primary schools... There was no Greek school, in which Homer was not read; cannot our popular schools, with their narrow range and their jejune alimentation in secular literature, do as much for the Bible as the Greek schools did for Homer?[81]

A century and half after Arnold asked that question, the answer to it would appear to be that, for deeply suspect reasons, state schools in England have not been able, or perhaps always willing, to do as he bid them. This is despite the attempt by framers of the 1988 Education Reform Act to safeguard authentic religious education in state schools. The overall consequence has arguably been to lead to their becoming the blackboard jungles that so many of them are today.[82]

Clearly, those growing up within families and neighbourhoods in which there is little trace of culture, religious or secular, are less likely to acquire from their schooling any interest in or taste for culture than those who grow up in more orderly and cultured domestic environments. Yet, unless schools make its nurturance among their most central priorities, the hold of culture upon even the most privileged is liable to weaken, as are habits of probity and civility. It was partly because Arnold considered culture such an effective moralising and civilising force that he valued it so. He wrote:

> ... the use of culture is that it helps us, by means of its spiritual standard of perfection, to regard wealth as but machinery and... really... perceive and feel that it is so. If it were not for this purging effect wrought upon our minds by culture, the whole world... would inevitably belong to the Philistines... And thus culture begets a dissatisfaction which is of the highest value in stemming the common tide of men's thoughts in a wealthy and industrial community, and which saves the future... even if it cannot save the present.[83]

The value of culture, for Arnold, went far beyond its capacity to serve as a moralising and civilising agent. He also valued it as much for what he considered to be its unique capacity to satisfy a powerful need that he posited in human beings. This need was for 'relating what we have learnt and known to the sense which we have in us for [morally good] conduct and to our sense for beauty.' [84] Other than to remark on the unique capacity of humane literature to satisfy this need, Arnold refrained from claiming to know, and hence from attempting to explain, how it was able to do so. The Edwardian classicist R.W. Livingstone was not so reticent. In a chapter entitled 'Physical Science and the Humanities' in his 1916 *Defence of Classical Education*, Livingstone observed:

> Imaginative literature in prose or poetry helps us... to see the world with imagination...That is why literature holds so important a place in education. It is a country where the light of imagination is continual, and all things are

illuminated by it... It is the world we know, inhabited by the men and women around us... Only, since we are not poets, our eyes have beheld, and we have not known the meaning of what we saw. But the poet sees the secret beauty and inner significance of things... We are happier, wiser better, for being taught thus to see the world... So instead of handing over our youth wholly... to science... we hand him over to literature, to the prophets of humanity, in the hope we may learn to see the world as they saw it, and catch something of their joy, nobility and inspiration.[85]

It was because of its unique capacity, not just to moralise people, but also to suggest to them ways in which to find the world a place of beauty as well as a source of inspiration for virtue, that Arnold valued culture as much as he did. He believed modern science, particularly Darwin's theory of evolution, had permanently discredited all religion in all its pre-modern forms. Yet he also believed that humans still retained, and always would, a need for some overall view of the world and their place within it that traditional religion had been so well able to satisfy in pre-modern times. Arnold believed that, within the body of great literature and art with which he equated culture, there could always be found the wherewithal with which to satisfy this powerful human need. It was because of his belief in its unique capacity to satisfy this need within conditions of modernity that Arnold so valued the nurturance of culture within young persons, and considered that to be the true purpose and rationale of formal education.

The predominantly literary and humanistic conception of culture Arnold had articulated in *Culture and Anarchy* was to be subject to public criticism from his friend Thomas Huxley. In an address delivered at the opening of Joseph Mason College in Birmingham in October 1880, Huxley accused Arnold of having espoused a one-sided conception of culture that undervalued the contribution to it made by science.[86] In 1882, Arnold responded to that criticism in a Rede lecture delivered at Cambridge under the title 'Literature and Science'.[87] In this lecture, Arnold defended himself against Huxley by pointing out that, within the expression 'the best that has been thought and said in the world', he had always intended to be included 'what in modern times has been thought and said by the great observers and knowers of nature'.[88] At the same time, Arnold also remained insistent that the humanities were able to meet a human need the sciences never could. He observed:

... the best that has been thought and uttered in the world... the art and poetry and eloquence of men who lived, perhaps, long ago [and] who had the most limited natural knowledge... have in fact, not only the power of refreshing and delighting us, [but] ... also the power... of fortifying, and elevating, and quickening, and... helping us to relate the results of modern science to our need for conduct [and] our need for beauty... The more that the results of science are frankly accepted... the more will the value of humane letters, and of art also, which is an utterance having a like kind of power... be felt and acknowledged, and their place in education be secured.[89]

Again, Arnold had not contended with the likes of educationists such as Martin Johnson, Ivor Goodson and Richard Pring. They all maintain that, in Arnold's sense, culture has always been considered to be the special preserve and possession of the few. The truth, however, is quite the reverse of what these critics have claimed. For, as Arnold was to remark:

... the idea which culture sets before us of perfection... is an idea which the new democracy needs far more than the idea of the blessedness of the franchise, or the wonderfulness of its own industrial performances... Culture... is not satisfied till we *all* come to a perfect man; it knows that the sweetness and light of the few must be imperfect until the raw and unkindled masses of humanity are touched with sweetness and light... [C]ulture... seeks to do away with classes; to make the best that has been thought and known in the world current everywhere; to make all men live in an atmosphere of sweetness and light, where they may use ideas... freely—nourished, and not bound by them... This is the *social idea*; and the men of culture are the true apostles of equality.[90]

Pring suggests Arnold considered culture to be the special preserve of a privileged elite; children of working-class background could only be initiated into it by being extricated from their families and social milieu. However, Arnold wanted culture in his sense disseminated as widely as possible throughout society. Although he believed that people differed in their susceptibility to its attractions, he also considered those potentially most susceptible could be found in every social class. If culture happened to be valued more highly by the more privileged social classes, this was only because hitherto they had enjoyed more exposure to it. Thus, Arnold observed: 'in each class there are born a certain number of natures with... a bent... for the pursuit of perfection... The number of those who will succeed in developing this happy instinct will be greater or smaller, in proportion to the force of the original instinct within them, and to the hindrance or encouragement which it meets from without.'[91]

In Arnold's view, practically no one was incapable of acquiring some degree of culture in his sense of the term by means of their receipt of a suitably pitched form of liberal education. This included even those whose education would never extend beyond elementary school. Thus, in his book about Prussian education, Arnold had observed:

> Every man is born with aptitudes... [for] knowledge... either by the road of studying man and his works, or by the road of studying nature and her works... As our public instruction gets a clearer view of its own functions, of the relation of the human spirit to knowledge, and of the entire circle of knowledge, it will certainly more learn to awaken in its pupils an interest in that entire circle, and less allow them to remain total strangers to any part of it... We are called to this knowledge by special aptitudes which are born to us; the grand thing in teaching is to have faith that some aptitudes of this kind every one has... and we should all have some notion... of the whole circle of knowledge.[92]

The stated purpose of the school curriculum proposed by Arnold in that work was to acquaint all secondary schoolchildren in England with the entire circle of knowledge needed for their receipt of (the first stage of) a liberal education. That proposed curriculum is strikingly similar to the National Curriculum in just the respects its critics have declared it to be elitist and exclusionary. It is now possible, however, to see it is they, not it or Matthew Arnold, who stand open to the charge of being elitist and exclusionary. For what we have been able to discover is that its purpose was to impart culture to all schoolchildren. In claiming the National Curriculum elitist and excessively academic in its original form, what its critics are effectively suggesting is that many normal children are insufficiently well-endowed intellectually to be able to acquire or benefit from culture. To make that suggestion is to write them off as incapable of benefiting from becoming acquainted with works, ideas and ideals that have been the source of delight and insight, consolation and inspiration, for countless generations from all backgrounds and social classes.

There is no good reason why culture in Arnold's sense should not be considered the rightful heritage of all schoolchildren in England into possession of which it should be the function of their schooling to bring them by means of a liberal education. All that stands in the way of realising this possibility are educationists and politicians seemingly bent upon using schools as venues in which to conduct class-wars and dubious experiments in social engineering. It is such opponents of liberal education, and not its advocates, who truly stand open to the accusation of harbouring an elitist and exclusionary view of education.

Without going so far as to suppose that everyone is in principle capable of benefiting from receipt of a (proper) university level education, there is no good reason to doubt that every child, un-afflicted by congenital abnormalities, is in principle capable of benefiting from receipt of a decent basic liberal education during their school years. The true educational challenge currently facing society in general and educators in particular is how best to ensure its provision to all who are capable of benefiting from it. As the great American apostle of liberal education Mortimer Adler once put it:

> Great inequalities in intelligence and other native endowments must be acknowledged; but to acknowledge them does not require us to adopt different aims in the schooling of the less gifted and in the schooling of the more gifted. A pint receptacle and a quart of gallon receptacle cannot hold the same quantity of liquid; but, while differing in the size of their capacity, they can all be filled to the brim; and if, furthermore, the very nature of their capacity craves the same kind of filling, then they are treated equally only when each is filled to the brim and each is filled with the same kind of substance, not the smaller receptacles with dirty water or skimmed milk and the larger receptacles with whole milk or rich cream…

> If whole milk or rich cream is too thick and viscous a substance easily to enter the narrow apertures at the top of the smaller receptacles, then we must invent the funnels needed for the infusion. Until a sustained and massive effort is made to discover the devices and methods that must be employed to give all children the same kind of treatment in school, motivated by the same aim and arising from a conviction that they are all educable in the same way, though not to the same degree, it is presumptuously dogmatic to assert that it cannot be done. All that can be said, in truth, is that it has not yet been done.[93]

State-funded schools in England seem finally on the point of being released from the straitjacket in which they have been confined for these last 20 years. Not least, that freedom is to be granted by means of a new generation of state-funded academies, freed from local authority control and other undue constraints. One can only hope that, in being granted that freedom, state-funded schools in England are not simultaneously relieved of their long-standing responsibility to endeavour to provide their pupils with a liberal education. This is a responsibility to which schools can best be held by the retention of a suitably academic

National Curriculum, but one much less detailed and prescriptive than has lately been in force.

9

Conclusion

There is much that can justly be said to be wrong with publicly-maintained education in England today. It suffers from an ill-conceived and counter-productive system of obligatory testing. Too much teaching in consequence has been made dull and routine to meet its demands. The curriculum has become over-crowded and cluttered by excessive demands, often made for extra-educational reasons. Too many class-rooms suffer from disorder and unruliness which their teachers lack adequate powers to deal with.

If the argument advanced in the present study has been correct, however, what would appear not to be wrong with education in England today is inclusion within the National Curriculum of the subjects whose study it prescribed when first introduced. As we have now seen, their originally intended purpose was jointly to provide (the preliminaries of) a liberal education. This is a form of education whose purpose and rationale was to nurture culture in its recipients, whose value, we have seen, was considered to reside in its uniquely civilising and humanising capacity.

Children and young persons are only capable of acquiring so much culture during the period of their compulsory education. Moreover, they vary in their individual receptivity to it. Possibly, those most receptive to it could be made to acquire much more by way of culture during their school years were England's publicly-maintained schools to become more selective than they have lately become. However, even a non-selective system of schooling should be able to provide a basic liberal education to all children whom adverse domestic circumstances had not rendered uneducable. This could be supplied by means of a suitably devised National Curriculum. It is a form of education increasingly being denied to English schoolchildren through ill-conceived hostility to the only kind of curriculum that can provide it.

There was and remains much that needs to be changed in the National Curriculum, even in the original form in which it was introduced. There is urgent need for it to give teachers and pupils greater scope for creativity. What does not need to change, however, are the subjects whose study it originally prescribed. As we have seen, their purpose was to impart to schoolchildren the entire circle of knowledge with which they need to be made acquainted during their formative years. They need such knowledge to have the wherewithal to lead as fulfilled lives as they might. Only those well acquainted with the various segments of that circle of knowledge know what children need to learn, and only they can teach it.

Unless the provision of liberal education is once again made the central purpose of state schools, it will increasingly become the exclusive preserve of the few privileged enough to attend independent schools. That is not the way of social progress, any more than it would be for independent schooling to be brought to an end in the name of social equality.

In having to choose whether to extend or further contract the provision of liberal education, by either reverting to or moving further away from the National Curriculum in its original form, this country faces as momentous a decision as any that it has ever faced in terms of the effects that it will have on future generations. It is to be hoped it has not yet become so servile and ill-educated a nation as not to know how it must choose to ensure its children, and its children's children, receive the only form of education that is able to provide them with the best prospects for as good and fulfilled lives as they can possibly enjoy—a liberal education.

Notes

Foreword

1   *New Yorker*, 12 September 1970.

2   White, J., *What schools are for and why*, London: Philosophy of Education Society of Great Britain, 2007, Impact No. 14, pp. 7-8.

3   Johnson, M., *Subject to Change: New thinking on the curriculum*, London: Association of Teachers and Lecturers, 2007, p. 16.

4   Hargreaves, D.H., *The Challenge for the Comprehensive School: Culture, curriculum and community*, London: Routledge & Kegan Paul, 1982, p. 185.

5   Ratzinger, J., *Milestones: Memoirs 1927-1977*, San Francisco: Ignatius Press, 1997, p. 23.

6   Eliot, T.S., *Notes Towards the Definition of Culture*, London: Faber and Faber, 1948, *passim*.

7   Pring, R., 'The Aim of Education: liberal or vocational?' in Pring, R., *Philosophy of Education: Aims, Theory, Common Sense, and Research*, London and New York: Continuum, 2004, p. 52.

8   Pring, R., 'Educating Persons' in Pring, *Philosophy of Education*, pp. 39-40.

9   Collier, P., *Wars, Guns and Votes: Democracy in dangerous places*, London: The Bodley Head, 2009, pp. 66-73.

Frontispiece

1   Aristotle, *The Politics*, Book 8, Chapter 3.

2   Eliot, T.S., 'A Commentary', *The Criterion*, vol. xiii, no. 52, April 1934.

1: How Schooling in England Went So Badly Wrong

1   Callaghan, J., 'Towards a national debate', Speech at the foundation stone-laying at Ruskin College, Oxford on 18 October 1976, *Guardian* 15 October 2001.

2   Gretton, J. and Jackson, M.N., *William Tyndale: Collapse of a school – or a system?*, London: George Allen and Unwin, 1976, pp. 18-19.

3   Gretton and Jackson, *William Tyndale*, p. 49.

4   The Auld Report quoted in Gretton and Jackson, *William Tyndale*, p. 120.

5   The Auld Report quoted in Gretton and Jackson, *William Tyndale*, p. 120.

6   Gretton and Jackson, *William Tyndale*, p. 121.

7   Callaghan, 'Towards a national debate'.

8   The present author has argued for the laudableness of this provision of the 1988 Education Reform Act in Conway, D., *Disunited Kingdom: How the government's community cohesion agenda undermines British identity and nationhood*, London: Civitas, 2009, See especially ch. 4 and the Appendix.

9   'Faking it. "Best ever" Key Stage 2 results—but how many children who reached Level 4 can actually read this sentence?' *Civitas*, http://www.civitas.org.uk/press/prcs61.php; de Waal, A., 'Testing is good—it's Sats tests that are bad', *Telegraph*, 20 December 2008.

10 Paton, G., 'Sats: Why are pupils sitting extra exams?', *Telegraph*, 4 August 2008.

11 Curry, B., Letter to *The Times*, 8 May 2009.

12 Paton, G., 'Primary schools "failing the brightest pupils"', *Telegraph*, 27 March 2009.

13 Robinson, A., 'A-levels are hard—in the wrong places', *Independent*, 15 August 2008.

14 Boston, K., 'Our early start on making children unfit for work', *Sunday Times*, 26 April 2009.

15 Boston, 'Our early start on making children unfit for work'.

16 Rose, J. *et al*, *Independent Review of the Primary Curriculum: Final Report*, DCSF Publications: Annesley, Nottingham, 2009; http://publications.teachernet.gov.uk/eOrderingDownload/Primary_curriculum _Report.pdf

17 The Diploma in Humanities and Social Sciences; http://www.ccskills.org.uk/ Qualifications/diplomainHumanities/tabid/85/Default.aspx

18 Henry, J., 'Axe traditional school subjects and standards will fall, warns top head', *Telegraph*, 16 May 2009.

19 Paton, G., 'Traditional school subjects "no longer fashionable"', *Telegraph*, 19 May 2009.

2: The National Curriculum as Culprit

1   Paton, G., 'Sex education to be "compulsory" in all state schools', *Telegraph*, 27 April 2009.

2   Brighouse, T., 'Accidents can happen', *QCA Futures*; http://www.qcda.gov.uk/libraryAssets/media/11475_brighouse_accidents_can_ happen.pdf

3 Brighouse, 'Accidents can happen', *QCA Futures*.

4 White, J., *What schools are for and why*, London: Philosophy of Education Society of Great Britain, 2007, Impact No. 14, p. 5.

5 White, *What schools are for and why*, pp. 7-8.

6 White, *What schools are for and why*, pp. 46-49 *passim*.

7 Johnson, M., *Subject to Change: New thinking on the curriculum* , London: Association of Teachers and Lecturers, 2007, p. 16.

8 Johnson, *Subject to Change*, p. 72.

9 Johnson, *Subject to Change*, p. 72.

10 Johnson, *Subject to Change*, pp. 101-102.

11 Johnson, *Subject to Change*, p. 103.

12 Johnson, *Subject to Change*, p. 146.

13 Quoted in Maw, J., 'National Curriculum Policy: coherence and progression?' in Lawton, D. and Chitty, C. (eds), *The National Curriculum*, London: Institute of Education, 1988, Bedford Way Papers, no. 33, 49-64, p. 50.

14 Swedish National Agency for Education, *National Evaluation of the Compulsory School in 2003: A summary main report*, Stockholm: Skolverket,, 2004, pp. 14-17 *passim*.

15 Swedish National Agency for Education, *Compulsory School: Syllabuses*, Skolverkert, Stockholm, 2009, p. 5.

16 Swedish National Agency for Education, Curriculum for the compulsory school system, the pre-school class and the leisure-time centre Lpo 94, Stockholm: Skolverket, 2006, p. 9.

17 Swedish National Agency for Education, *Compulsory School: Syllabuses*, p. 3.

18 The percentage figures, year on year, of eligible year 12 pupils who did not achieve a single A*-C grade in any GCSE subject are: 1997 (30%); 1998 (29%); 1999 (28%); 2000 (27%); 2001 (26%); 2002 (25%); 2003 (26%); 2004 (25%); 2005 (24%); 2006 (24%); 2007 (23%). See *Hansard*, written answers for 21 July 2008: col. 929w.

19 Green D., *Individualists Who Co-operate: Education and welfare reform befitting a free people*, London: Civitas, 2009, p. 84.

20 Green, *Individualists Who Co-operate*, p. 84.

21 Green, *Individualists Who Co-operate*, p. 85.

22 Green, *Individualists Who Co-operate*, p. 85.

23 Gretton, J. and Jackson, M.N., *William Tyndale: Collapse of a school – or a system?*, London: George Allen and Unwin, 1976, p. 112.

24 See MacEoin, D., *Music, Chess and Other Sins: Segregation, integration and Muslim schools in Britain*, London: Civitas, 2009, available online at: http://www.civitas.org.uk/pdf/MusicChessAndOtherSins.pdf

25 For having had my attention drawn to the problematic character of Waldorf Steiner schools and especially their being state-funded, I am indebted to a pair of postings on the 'Ministry of Truth' website (www.ministryoftruth.me.uk) by the pseudonymous blogger 'Unity': 'Fairies at the bottom of the schoolyard' *Ministry of Truth* website, 10 July 2009; and 'Pseudoscience—not a valid educational choice', *Ministry of Truth* website, 22 July 2009.

26 Ross, T., 'Tories to offer alternative state education at Montessori schools', *London Evening Standard*, 8 July 2009.

27 Simpson, P.V., 'Stockholm University ends Steiner teacher training', *The Local: Sweden's news in English*, 28 August 2008; http://www.thelocal.se/13944/20080826/

28 Simpson, 'Stockholm University ends Steiner teacher training'.

29 Simpson, 'Stockholm University ends Steiner teacher training'.

30 Simpson, 'Stockholm University ends Steiner teacher training'.

31 See Steiner Waldorf Schools Fellowship Directory; http://www.steinerwaldorf.org/steinerschoolslist.html

32 Woods, P., Ashley, M. and Woods, G., *Steiner Schools in England*, Research Report no. 645, Centre for Research in Education and Democracy, Faculty of Education, Bristol: University of the West, 2005.

33 Macmillan website: information about Woods. P.A. and Woods, G.J. (eds), *Alternative Education for the 21st Century*, Houndmills, Basingstoke: Palgrave Macmillan: 2008; http://us.macmillan.com/alternativeeducationforthe21stcentury

34 'What is Angelic Reiki?' Angelic Reiki Healing UK Information; http://www.angelicreiki.info/what_is_angelic_reiki

35 Woods, Ashley and Woods, *Steiner Schools in England*, p. 125.

36 *Hansard* Debates for 21 November 2007: Column 196; http://www.parliament.the-stationery-office.co.uk/pa/cm200708/cmhansrd/cm071121/debtext/71121-0005.htm

37 Scott, E.C., 'Waldorf Schools Teach Odd Science, Odd Evolution', National
    Centre for Science Education: Oakland, California, 1994, p. 2;
    http://www.waldorfcritics.org/active/articles/Eugenie_Scott_94.html

38 Peacock, A.T. and Wiseman, J., *Education for Democrats*, London: Institute of
    Economic Affairs, 1964, p. 27.

39 Blaug, M. and West, E.G., *Education: A framework for choice*, London: Institute of
    Economic Affairs, 1967, Readings in Political Economy 1, p. 43.

3: Some Common and Less Common Myths About the National Curriculum

1   Aldrich, R., 'The National Curriculum: an historical perspective' in Lawton, D.
    and Chitty, C. (eds), *The National Curriculum*, London: Institute of Education,
    1988, Bedford Way Papers, No. 22, 21-33, pp. 22-23.

2   Aldrich, 'The National Curriculum', pp. 30-31.

3   White, J., 'An Unconstitutional National Curriculum', in Lawton, D. and Chitty,
    C. (eds), *The National Curriculum*, 113-122, p. 117.

4   White, 'An Unconstitutional National Curriculum', p. 117.

5   White, 'An Unconstitutional National Curriculum', p. 117.

6   White, J., 'Introduction' in White, J. (ed.), *Rethinking the School Curriculum:
    Values, aims and purposes*, London and New York: Routledge-Falmer, 2004, p. 6.

7   Goodson, I., 'The Exclusive Pursuit of Social Inclusion', *Forum*, vol. 47, numbers
    2 and 3, 2005, 145-150, p. 148.

8   Goodson, 'The Exclusive Pursuit of Social Inclusion', pp. 148-49.

9   Goodson, 'The Exclusive Pursuit of Social Inclusion', p. 147.

10 Goodson, 'The Exclusive Pursuit of Social Inclusion', pp. 149-50.

11 Hewlett, M., 'Educating Young People for the 21st Century: Constructing an
    Aims-Led Curriculum', Nuffield Review Working Paper 47, Nuffield Review
    website, December 2008, p. 26;
    http://www.nuffield14-19review.org.uk/files/documents204-1.pdf

12 White, J., 'The Puritan Origins of the 1988 School Curriculum in England', in
    Moore, A. (ed.) *Schooling, Society and Curriculum*, London and New York:
    Routledge Taylor and Francis Group, 2006, 43 - 59, p. 58.

13 White, J., *Towards an Aims-led Curriculum*, QCA Futures, QCA website. undated.

14 White, 'The Puritan Origins of the 1988 School Curriculum in England', p. 45.

15 White, 'The Puritan Origins of the 1988 School Curriculum in England', pp. 47-50 *passim* (my emphasis).

16 White, 'The Puritan Origins of the 1988 School Curriculum in England', pp. 54-56 *passim*.

17 White, 'The Puritan Origins of the 1988 School Curriculum in England', p. 59.

4: On the Alleged Puritan Origins of the National Curriculum

1 Watson, F., *The Beginnings of the Teaching of Modern Subjects in England*, London: Sir Isaac Pitman and Sons, 1909, p. 139.

2 Turnbull, G., *Observations upon Liberal Education*, Indianapolis: Liberty Fund, 2003, Moore Jr., T.O. (ed.), Editorial Introduction, p. xv.

3 Trafton, J. and Ryken, L., 'Richard Baxter and the English Puritans: Did you know?', *Christianity Today*, 1 January 2006.

4 Hooykaas, R., *Religion and the Rise of Modern Science*, Edinburgh and London: Scottish Academic Press, first published 1972, paperback edition with corrections, 1973, pp. 99-100.

5 Hooykaas, *Religion and the Rise of Modern Science*, pp. 104 and 106.

6 Kristeller, P.O., 'The Modern System of the Arts' in Kristeller, P.O., *Renaissance Thought and the Arts*, Princeton, N.J: Princeton University Press, 1990, 163-227, p. 187.

7 Graves, F.P., *Peter Ramus and the Educational Reforms of the Sixteenth Century*, New York: Macmillan, 1912, pp. 204-18 *passim*.

8 Morgan, J., *Godly Learning: Puritan attitudes towards reason, learning and education,1560-1640*, Cambridge: Cambridge University Press, 1986.

9 White, J., 'The Puritan Origins of the 1988 School Curriculum in England', in Moore, A. (ed.) *Schooling, Society and Curriculum*, London and New York: Routledge Taylor and Francis Group, 2006, 43 - 59, p. 50.

10 Hooykaas, *Religion and the Rise of Modern Science*, p. 148.

11 Hooykaas, *Religion and the Rise of Modern Science*, p. 147.

5: The 1904 Regulations as Alleged Source of the National Curriculum

1 Baker, K., *The Turbulent Years: My life in politics*, London: Faber and Faber, 1993, p. 193.

2   Baker, *The Turbulent Years*, p. 193.

3   Baker, *The Turbulent Years*, p. 193.

4   Norwood, C. and Hope, A.H., *The Higher Education of Boys in England*, London: John Murray, 1909.

5   Board of Education, *Report of the Consultative Committee on Secondary Education with Special Reference to Grammar Schools and Technical High Schools*, London: HMSO, 1939, ch.1 section 37; (web-based version) http://www.dg.dial.pipex.com/documents/docs2/spens01.shtml

6: The True Source of the National Curriculum

1   Young, R.F., 'Note by the secretary in the development of the conception of general liberal education', Appendix ll of *Secondary Education* (The Spens Report), London: HMSO, 1938, web-based version, p. 7.

2   Arnold, M., 'A French Eton or Middle-Class Education and the State' in Arnold, M., *The Works of Matthew Arnold*, vol. Xll, London: Macmillan, 1904, p. 24.

3   Arnold, M., 'Higher Schools and Universities in Germany' in Arnold, M., *The Works of Matthew Arnold*, vol. Xll, London: Macmillan, 1904, pp. 407-14 *passim*.

7: Liberal Education as the Purpose of the National Curriculum

1   Arnold, M., 'Higher Schools and Universities in Germany' in Arnold, M., *The Works of Matthew Arnold*, vol. Xll, London: Macmillan, 1904, p. 399.

2   Arnold, M., 'A French Eton or Middle-Class Education and the State' in Arnold, M., *The Works of Matthew Arnold*, vol. Xll, London: Macmillan, 1904, p. 3.

3   Arnold, 'Higher Schools and Universities in Germany', p. 399.

4   Arnold, 'Higher Schools and Universities in Germany', pp. 386-87.

5   Morant, R., Introduction to the 1904 *Elementary School Code* quoted in Allen, B.M., *Sir Robert Morant: A great public servant*, London: Macmillan, 1934, pp. 211-212.

6   Allen, *Sir Robert Morant*, pp. 213-14.

7   Allen, *Sir Robert Morant*, p. 214.

8   Morant, R., Prefatory Memorandum' to the 'Regulations for Secondary Schools, 1904', in Sylvester, D.W. and MacIure, S. (eds), *Educational Documents: England and Wales*, first published 1965, London: Taylor and Frances, 2006, pp. 156-59, pp. 157-58.

9 McCulloch, G., *Cyril Norwood and the Ideal of Secondary Education*, Houndmills, Basingstoke: Palgrave Macmillan, 2007, p. 156 and p. 2.

10 Norwood, C. and Hope, A.H., *The Higher Education of Boys in England*, London: John Murray, 1909, p. 283

11 Norwood and Hope, *The Higher Education of Boys in England*, pp. 283-87 *passim*.

12 Norwood and Hope, *The Higher Education of Boys in England*, p. 295.

13 Fisher, H.A.L., Speech in the House of Commons, August 1917, quoted in Bourne, R. and MacArthur, B., *The Struggle for Education, 1870-1970*, London: Schoolmaster Publishing Company, 1970, p. 67.

14 Fisher, H.A.L., *The Place of the University in National Life*, Barnett House Papers No. 4, London, Edinburgh: Humphrey Milford and Oxford University Press, 1919, p. 11.

15 Board of Education, *The Education of the Adolescent: Report of the Consultative Committee* (the Hadow Report), London: HMSO, 1927, p. iv.

16 Board of Education, *The Education of the Adolescent*, p. xxiii.

17 Board of Education, *The Education of the Adolescent*, p. xxiv.

18 Board of Education, *The Education of the Adolescent*, p. 174.

19 Board of Education, *The Education of the Adolescent*, pp. 188-89.

20 Norwood, C., *The English Tradition of Education*, London: John Murray, 1929, p. 87.

21 Norwood, *The English Tradition of Education*, p. 89.

22 Norwood, *The English Tradition of Education*, pp. 89-91 passim.

23 Norwood, Norwood, *The English Tradition of Education*, pp. 307-308.

24 Norwood, *The English Tradition of Education*, pp. 311-312.

25 Sampson, G., *English for the English: A chapter on national education*, First published 1921, New Edition 1952, Cambridge: Cambridge University Press, 1952, p.1 and pp.3-4.

26 Sampson, *English for the English*, p. 4.

27 Sampson, *English for the English*, p. 7.

28 Sampson, *English for the English*, pp. 11-12.

29 Sampson, *English for the English*, pp. 14-15.

30 Sampson, *English for the English*, p. 34.

31 Sampson, *English for the English*, p. 18.

32 Sampson, *English for the English*, p. 27.

33 Sampson, *English for the English*, p. 29.

34 Sampson, *English for the English*, p. 31.

35 Sampson, *English for the English*, p. 38.

36 Sampson, *English for the English*, pp. 41-42.

37 Sampson, *English for the English*, p. 105.

38 Sampson, *English for the English*, pp.104-05.

39 Mill, J.S., 'Autobiography' in Lerner, M. (ed.), *Essential Works of John Stuart Mill*, New York: Bantam Books, 1965, p. 22.

40 Wolf, A., *Does Education Matter? Myths about Education and Education Growth*, London: Penguin, 2002, p. 254.

41 Sampson, *English for the English*, pp. 44-45.

42 Richard Tawney lecture delivered at York in March 1931. Quoted in Sadler, M., *Liberal Education for Everybody*, London: The Lindsey Press, 1932, pp. 32-33.

43 Sadler, *Education for Everybody*, p. 37.

44 Sadler, *Education for Everybody*, p. 33.

45 Sadler, *Education for Everybody*, pp. 36-39 passim.

46 Norwood and Hope, *The Higher Education of Boys in England*, p. v.

47 McCulloch, *Cyril Norwood and the Ideal of Secondary Education*, p. 142. The quoted passage of what Norwood said to Butler at their meeting on 27 November 1941 is from Butler, R.A., 'Note on meeting with Cyril Norwood, November 27, 1941', Board of Education papers, ED.12/478.

48 Board of Education, *Curriculum and Examinations in Secondary Schools* (The Norwood Report), London: HMSO, 1943, ch. 1; online version, p. 5. http://www.dg.dial.pipex.com/documents/docs2/norwood.

49 Board of Education, *Curriculum and Examinations in Secondary Schools*, ch. 8, p. 17.

50 Board of Education, *Curriculum and Examinations in Secondary Schools*, ch. 8., p. 17.

51 Board of Education, *Curriculum and Examinations in Secondary Schools*, ch. 8, pp. 17-18.

52 Board of Education, *Curriculum and Examinations in Secondary Schools*, ch. 3, p. 5.

53 Paton, G., 'Indiscipline soars at larger schools', *Telegraph*, 1 April 2007.

54 Paton, 'Indiscipline soars at larger schools'.

55 Board of Education, *Curriculum and Examinations in Secondary Schools*, ch. 8, pp. 2-3.

56 Department of Education press release, 7 July 1988; quoted in Pring, R. *et al.*, *Education for All: The future of education and training for 14-19 year olds*, London and New York: Routledge, 2009, p. 108.

57 Baker, K., *The Turbulent Years: My life in politics*, London: Faber and Faber, 1993, pp. 200-01.

58 Baker, *The Turbulent Years*, pp. 201-02.

59 Connell, W.F., *The Educational Thought and Influence of Matthew Arnold*, Westport, Connecticut: Cornwood Press, 1971, p. 184.

60 Arnold, M., 1852-1892, Marvin, F.S. (ed.), *Reports on Elementary Schools*, London: HMSO, 1908, quoted in Connell, *The Educational Thought and Influence of Matthew Arnold*, pp. 184-85.

61 Arnold, *Reports on Elementary Schools*, pp. 186-87, quoted in Connell, *The Educational Thought and Influence of Matthew Arnold*, p.183.

8: The Meaning, Origin and Rationale of Liberal Education

1 Pring, R. *et al.*, *Education for All: The future of education and training for 14-19 year olds*, London and New York: Routledge, 2009.

2 Pring, R., 'The aim of education: liberal or vocational?' in Pring, R., *Philosophy of Education: Aims, Theory, Common Sense, and Research*, London and New York: Continuum, 2004.

3 Pring, 'The aim of education: liberal or vocational?', pp. 50-51.

4 Pring, 'The aim of education', pp. 58-59.

5 Pring, 'The aim of education', pp. 59-60.

6 Pring, 'The aim of education', p. 57.

7   Newman, J.H., *The Idea of a University: Defined and illustrated*, London: Longman, Green and Co., 1902, pp. 107-09.

8   Connor, W.R., 'Liberal Arts Education in the Twenty-First Century', American Academy for Liberal Education, 1998, Occasional Papers # 2, p. 4; http://www.aale.org/pdf/connor.pdf

9   Plutarch, *Cimon*, translated by Dryden, J., Internet Classics archive; http://classics.mit/edu/Putarch/cimon.html

10 Muir, J., 'Is our history of educational philosophy mostly wrong?: The Case of Isocrates', *Theory and Research in Education*, vol. 3 (2), 2005, 165-195.

11 Isocrates, *Panegyricus*, 4. 47-49 in Norlin, G. (ed.), Isocrates, *Isocrates with an English translation*, Cambridge, Mass: Harvard University Press,1980; http://www.perseus.tufts.edu/hopper/text?doc=Perseus%3Atext%3A1999.01.014 4%3Aspeech%3D4%3Asection%3D49

12 See Joint Association of Classical Teachers, *The World of Athens: An introduction to classical Athenian culture*, Cambridge: Cambridge University Press, 1984, pp. 211-12.

13 Aristotle, *The Politics*, Harmondsworth: Penguin Books, 1981, revised edition, Book 8, ch. 3, pp. 456-57.

14 See Conway, D., *The Rediscovery of Wisdom: From here to antiquity in quest of Sophia*, Houndmills, Basingstoke: Macmillan, 2000.

15 See Kimball, B.A., *Orators & Philosophers: A history of the idea of liberal education*, New York and London: Teachers College Press, 1986.

16 Entry on 'Advocates' in the *Penny Cyclopaedia of the Society for the Diffusion of Useful Knowledge*, vol. 1, London: Charles Knight, 1833, p. 135.

17 'Why do barristers wear robes?', *Western Australian Bar Association Review*, vol. 29, Issue 1, June 2005; http://www.nswbar.asn.au/docs/about/what_is/gowns.pdf

18 Pring, R., 'The aim of education', p. 60.

19 Pring, R., 'The Common School' in Halstead, M. and Haydon, G. (eds), *The Common School and the Comprehensive Ideal: A defence by Richard Pring with complementary essays*, Oxford: Wiley-Blackwell, 2008, 1-19, pp. 11-12.

20 Newman, *The Idea of a University*, p. 122.

21 Pring *et al.*, *Education for All*, p. 19.

22 Newman, *The Idea of a University*, p. 129.

23 Newman, *The Idea of a University*, p. 135.

24 Newman, *The Idea of a University*, p. 139.

25 Newman, *The Idea of a University*, p. 137.

26 Newman, *The Idea of a University*, p. 139.

27 Newman, *The Idea of a University*, pp. 141-43.

28 Newman, *The Idea of a University*, p. 143.

29 Pring, 'The Common School', p. 11.

30 Newman, *The Idea of a University*, pp. 147-48.

31 Newman, *The Idea of a University*, pp. 148-50.

32 Entry for "poetry", *The Shorter Oxford English Dictionary*, Oxford: Oxford University Press, 1973, p. 1615.

33 Newman, *The Idea of a University*, p. 227.

34 Newman, *The Idea of a University*, p. 233.

35 Paton, G., 'Thousands of pupils "drop out of school at 14"', *Telegraph*, 23 February 2009.

36 Shepherd, J., 'Truancy on the rise in England as 4.3.m days of school are missed', *Guardian*, 18 June 2009.

37 Pring, 'The common school', p. 7.

38 Mill, J.S., 'Inaugural Address Delivered to the University of St. Andrews', 1 February 1867 in *Collected Works of John Stuart Mill*, vol. XXl, *Essays on Equality, Law and Education* (ed.) Robson, J.M., Toronto and London: Routledge and Kegan Paul, 1984, 215-258, p. 219; http://oll.libertyfund.org/index.php?option=com_staticxt&staticfile=show.php&title=255&search=%22The+proper+function+of+an+University%22&chapter=21681&layout=html#a_809560

39 Mill, 'Inaugural Address', p. 219.

40 Mill, 'Inaugural Address', p. 219.

41 Mill, 'Inaugural Address', p. 221.

42 Mill, 'Inaugural Address', p. 218.

43 Mill, 'Inaugural Address', p. 224.

44 Mill, 'Inaugural Address', pp. 247-48.

45 Pring, R., 'Educating persons' in Pring,. R., *Philosophy of Education*, 26-41, p. 28.

46 Pring, 'Educating persons', p. 28.

47 Clark, L., '2,200 pupils sent home every day as violent behaviour in class reaches record levels', *Daily Mail*, 24 June 2008.

48 Paton, G., 'Hundreds of children under five suspended from school in a year', *Telegraph*, 6 November 2008.

49 Brady, B. and Owen, J., 'Pupils as young as six excluded for taking knives into school', *Independent*, 15 February 2009.

50 'Pupils' behaviour "has worsened"', *Lancashire Evening Post*, 6 April 2009.

51 Waite, L.J. and Gallagher, M., *The Case for Marriage: Why Married People are Happier, Healthier , and Better Off Financially*, New York: Broadway Book, 2000, p. 125.

52 Mill, 'Inaugural Address', p. 251.

53 Mill, 'Inaugural Address', pp. 253-55 *passim*.

54 Paton, G., 'Labour's school reforms have destroyed English, says ATL head Mary Bousted', *Telegraph*, 9 April 2009.

55 Mill, J.S., 'Utilitarianism' in Mill, J.S., *On Liberty and Other Essays*, Gray, J. (ed.), Oxford and New York: Oxford University Press,1991, p. 141.

56 Mill, 'Utilitarianism', p. 145.

57 Mill, 'Autobiography' *Essential Works of John Stuart Mill*, Lerner, M. (ed.), New York, Toronto and London: Bantam Books, 1965, p. 91.

58 Mill, 'Utilitarianism', p. 145.

59 Leavis, F.R., 'The "Great Books" and A Liberal Education' in Leavis, F.R., *The Critic as Anti-Philosopher*, Chicago: Ivan R. Dee, 1998, 156-70, p. 168.

60 Pring, 'The aim of education', p. 52.

61 Pring, 'The common school', p. 7.

62 Pring, 'Educating persons', pp. 39-40.

63 Pring *et al.*, *Education for All*, pp. 71-73. [I have transposed the order of some sentences in this quotation.]

64 See Popper, K.R., *Conjectures and Refutations: The growth of scientific knowledge*, Fourth Edn, London and Henley: Routledge and Kegan Paul, 1972, esp. ch. 10, 'Truth, Rationality, and the Growth of Scientific Knowledge'.

65 Arnold, M., Preface to the 1869 edition of 'Culture and Anarchy' in Arnold, M., *Culture and Anarchy and Other Writings*, Collini, S. (ed.), Cambridge: Cambridge University Press, 1993, p. 190.

66 Arnold, 'Culture and Anarchy', p. 85, editorial footnote.

67 Arnold, 'Culture and Anarchy', pp. 83-89 *passim*.

68 Arnold, 'Culture and Anarchy', pp. 180-82 *passim*.

69 See Davies, C., *The Strange Death of Moral Britain*, New Brunswick and London: Transaction Publishers, 2006, ch. 1.

70 Davies, *The Strange Death of Moral Britain*, pp. 3-6 passim.

71 See Himmelfarb, G., *The De-moralization of Society: From Victorian virtues to modern values*, London: IEA Health and Welfare Unit, 1995. Ch. ll.

72 Himmelfarb, *The De-moralization of Society*, pp. 222-223.

73 Himmelfarb, *The De-moralization of Society*, p. 223.

74 Tibbetts, G., 'Most children of British mothers born out of wedlock', *Telegraph*, 11 July 2008.

75 Brown, C.G., *The Death of Christian Britain: Understanding secularisation 1800-2000*, London and New York: Routledge, 2001, p. 1.

76 Davies, *The Strange Death of Moral Britain*, pp. 27-28.

77 Coates, S., 'Inner-city violence is taking us to the wire, say Tories', *The Times*, 25 August 2009.

78 Arnold, M. quoted in Connell, W.F., *The Educational Thought and Influence of Matthew Arnold*, Westport, Connecticut: Greenwood Press, 1971, p. 141.

79 Arnold, M., *Literature and Dogma* (1873) quoted in Connell, *The Educational Thought and Influence of Matthew Arnold*, p. 144 and p.146.

80 Arnold, M., *Popular Education of France, with Notices of that of Holland and Switzerland* (1861), quoted in Connell, *The Educational Thought and Influence of Matthew Arnold*, p. 152.

81 Arnold, M., 'Report on Elementary Schools' (1869), quoted in Connell, *The Educational Thought and Influence of Matthew Arnold*, pp. 153-54.

82 See Conway, D., *Disunited Kingdom: How the government's community cohesion agenda undermines British identity and nationhood*, Civitas: London, 2009, Part One.

83 Arnold, 'Culture and Anarchy', p. 65.

84 Arnold, M, 'Literature and Science', Arnold, M., 'Literature and Science', Rede Lecture, Cambridge 1882. Quotations are from the later version of this lecture given as an address by Arnold on a tour of America in 1883; web version, http://www.chass.utoronto.ca/~ian/arnold.htm, p. 5.

85 Livingstone, R.W., *A Defence of Classical Education*, London: Macmillan, 1916, pp. 43-50 passim.

86 Huxley, T.H., 'Science and Culture', lecture delivered at the opening of Mason College in 1880; http://www.bluepete.com/iteratuyre/Essays/Best/HuxleyScienceCult...

87 Arnold, 'Literature and Science', pp. 7-8.

88 Arnold, 'Literature and Science', p.4.

89 Arnold, 'Literature and Science', pp. 7-8.

90 Arnold, 'Culture and Anarchy', pp. 76-79.

91 Arnold, 'Culture and Anarchy', pp. 109-110.

92 Arnold, M., 'Higher Schools and Universities in Germany' in Arnold, M., *The Works of Matthew Arnold*, vol. Xll, London: Macmillan, 1904, p. 399.

93 Adler, M.J., 'The Schooling of a People,' in Adler, M.J., *Reforming Education: The opening of the American mind*, Van Dorn, G. (ed.), New York and London: Macmillan, 1988, 114-138, pp. 133-34.